FEEDING KIDS CAN OFTEN FEEL LIKE CLIMBING A MOUNTAIN, and sometimes like an endless series of rejections and failures. With picky eating preferences changing at every turn, meals that were a mainstay one week are inexplicably pushed aside when they hit the table the next. Because kids don't care about what they're serving at the new It Restaurant, the food fads of the year, or how long you spend in the kitchen—either they like what they're eating or they'll let you know about it! But surely chefs, with all of their accolades, awards, and years of experience don't go through this too . . . do they? What food writer Joanna Fox discovered might surprise you: it turns out we're all in the same boat, even Canada's top culinary professionals from coast to coast.

Inside *Little Critics*, you'll find out how our top chefs please even the most suspicious, judgmental, or fastidious of early eaters, with recipes including **Jeremy Charles's** go-to stew, **Suzanne Barr's** Cauliflower Cheese Bake, **Susur Lee's** favourite childhood chicken, **Danny Smiles's** Italian family dinner, **Dyan Solomon's** Green Hulk Risotto, **Vikram Vij's** Butter Chicken Schnitzel, **Ryusuke Nakagawa's** Cheesy Chicken Katsu, **Billy Alexander's** Frybread Stuffed Pizza, **Chuck Hughes's** Pappardelle Pesto, **Michael Smith's** showstopper pancakes, **Tara O'Brady's** hearty Oatmeal Waffles, and **Anna Olson's** Gourmet Goo Skillet Brownies.

Little Critics is chock-full of ideas for every kind of meal, with easy-to-follow recipes for breakfast and brunch; vegetarian, fish, and meat mains; soups, snacks, and sides; and desserts and drinks too. With food this good, even the adults will be asking for more.

Little Critics

Clockwise from top left:
Candy Sangria, page 241;
Horchata, page 243;
Strawberry Mint Mocktail,
page 242

Little Critics

What Canadian Chefs Cook for Kids

(AND KIDS ACTUALLY EAT)

Joanna Fox

appetite
by RANDOM HOUSE

Appetite by Random House® and colophon are registered trademarks of Penguin Random House LLC.

Library and Archives Canada Cataloguing in Publication is available upon request.

ISBN: 978-0-525-61150-9
eBook ISBN: 978-0-525-61151-6

Photography by Dominique Lafond
Photos on pages 4, 30, 31, 88, 89, 91, 124, 125, 212, 213, 220, 221, 237, 248, 253, 254, 255, and 256 by Maya Visnyei; and on pages 60, 61, 84, and 253 by Viranlly Liemena
Book design by Talia Abramson
Printed in Canada

Published in Canada by Appetite by Random House®, a division of Penguin Random House Canada Limited.

www.penguinrandomhouse.ca

10 9 8 7 6 5 4 3 2 1

appetite by RANDOM HOUSE | Penguin Random House Canada

Michael Smith's Country Inn Pancakes with Maple Syrup, page 17

This book is dedicated to my parents, who had to live through years of my picky eating, and to my son, who is putting me through the exact same thing.

Contents

Vegetarian Mains

Fish & Meat Mains

Desserts & Drinks

Foreword

Once you've gathered the accolades, as they call them. Once you've been in print and on the screen, enjoying the rarest crus and bloodiest cuts with the bishops of gastronomes. Once you've toured all coasts for since-forgotten collabs. Once you've shaken the culinary tree till all the stars have piled on you. Then, when you least expect it, comes the critic you fear the most. It's no longer the newspaper reviewers who hold the power, whose every word hits like a cannonball in the hull of your skills. No, not them. Now the one you fear is the fruit of your loins—the person you stopped riding motorcycles for.

No one more than a culinary professional approaches kids' food with such great ambition. We make firm and unshakable statements: my kids will eat everything we eat; we will take them everywhere with us. At not even 2 months old, there's already blanquette aux morilles, puréed and frozen into perfect cubes, awaiting their first gourmet experience. But the proclamations never materialize. Your child eats anchovies once. In front of your in-laws—for the long-awaited display of genetically fated finesse—they prefer by far the taste of their boogers to the banquet spread out in front of them, like the frog that won't sing in front of the agent. Meanwhile, the freezer takes its toll on that blanquette!

To aid this cause, the internet is filled with the ruins of parenthood start-ups that once sounded great but failed to deliver the tiny gastro-nauts they promised. And so time marches on, until one day—when these little squirts eventually get bigger—it gets better. For the in-between time, for the years that stretch ahead, you have this resource.

I would have never thought that a book on such a topic would make so much sense, but then I had kids. I've known Joanna for 15 years, and I know that she is a great writer. I also know that with her approach, skills, and talent, this cookbook won't end up amongst the ruins.

Fred Morin

Introduction

Growing up, I was a picky eater. Everything my parents put on my plate was scrutinized, prodded, poked, and moved around, and then, often, strategically made its way under the table and discreetly onto the floor. Like a lot of kids, I was a creature of habit and wanted the same things, over and over, every day. I think I had a ham sandwich on baguette with mustard every day for lunch throughout my elementary years (and I'm surprised I don't glow in the dark from the amount of nitrates I've consumed). As I got older, I slowly became more adventurous, but it was only when I started to travel the world and, while travelling, worked in hospitality that I began to really broaden my horizons. There's something about the restaurant industry and being around food and food people that pushes you to just go for it. By the time I landed a job waitressing at Joe Beef in my late 20s, the floodgates were wide open.

A lot of the picky eaters out there tend to become the biggest lovers of food (and some just become adult picky eaters). I fell into the former category and embarked on a culinary journey that had me doing everything from food styling (which I was terrible at, for the record) to working on cooking shows, writing cookbooks, waitressing, making food guides, reviewing restaurants, and, most of all, cooking like crazy. I was that person who filled their teeny tiny apartment bathtub with ice and snow crab for dinner parties. I would make my own tortillas for 20-person taco nights and spend 3 days slow-cooking a pork shoulder. I had boundless energy for experimenting and discovering new dishes, and threw the most elaborate meals imaginable for anyone who wanted to crowd around my massive dining room table, which was always the centrepiece crammed into every place I lived.

And then, one day, I had a baby. Which turned elaborate meals into me standing up while eating whatever was in the fridge, or picking up and eating what my son threw to the floor. My dinner parties fizzled when I realized I now wanted to end them well before my pre-baby-life 9 pm start times. My usual three courses turned into a panicked one-pot meal, my open invitations and "more the merrier" joie de vivre were cut off at a strict six topper, max. How did I use to do this? Where had all my energy come from? And what happened to me?

My son was actually the best thing that happened to me, besides meeting my partner, his father, years before. And eventually, as my son started to eat more food—and a variety, at that—meals became a bit more normal, I had more time to cook, and I started to make more interesting dinners, regaining energy and confidence. And my son was eating everything. I was so proud. I mean, his mother had such

a developed palate, so it only made sense . . . Until one day, probably around his third birthday, he turned on me. Or rather, he turned into me. Everything was "no" or "ugh" or "yuck," and all my usual go-tos were rejected, one by one. Eggs, pasta, chicken, cheese, fish, rice, vegetables, mashed potatoes, even French fries—nothing would stick.

And then I realized something. I had a lot of chef friends, and quite a few of them now had kids. I wondered what they were feeding their own kids and if their kids were as picky as mine. One of the amazing things about children is that they have an uncanny ability to level the playing field. If Chuck Hughes's kids were telling him their dinner "could be better," I felt better. When Fred Morin's son told him his food sucked, I have to admit, it made me kind of happy. Because if these top chefs weren't able to please their kids, the pressure was way off me. All of a sudden, we were all in the same boat. The truth was, we were all at the mercy of these tough little critics.

That being said, there was always a "but." There was always that dish, that fail-safe recipe that, no matter what, managed to please the peanut gallery. Just like when I was young there were these sweet, sticky, salty soy chicken drumsticks my mom made from an old issue of *Canadian Living* that I loved. And I would be so happy every time she made them, knowing I wouldn't have to, God forbid, eat something gross. And it was the same thing for every chef I spoke to. Each one had that slam-dunk recipe that their children, or the children in their lives, would always eat—or even that they remembered eating when they were young.

So I decided to do something helpful for all the parents and caregivers out there, all the godparents and uncles and aunts and cousins and friends who ever had to cook for children. I asked some of Canada's best culinary minds, from coast to coast to coast, what they made for the kids in their lives. And while I was at it, I also wanted to create a cookbook that would help teach children and parents about the diversity of our country and its people, and how rich and amazing our food culture really is. What better way to understand what Canada is today than through the lens of its many different recipes and culinary traditions?

All of the incredibly generous chefs in this cookbook gave me their best recipes so that you would have plenty of options come mealtime to put a smile on your kids' faces and show them that there is so much to discover through food. And who knows, those picky eaters might surprise you with what they like—I know mine did.

Breakfast & Brunch

If there has to be a godsend in the daily scheme of kids' meals, it's breakfast and brunch. It's far easier to get that elusive two-thumbs-up rating with a stack of pancakes or waffles than with, say, a side of steamed broccoli (two thumbs down). I was extremely lucky in this department, as my son miraculously took to being obsessed with avocado on toast—albeit with the crusts cut off, but beggars can't be choosers here, I'll take what I can get (fibre, protein, good fat!). It's also nice to make a fun breakfast on weekends, and since sleeping in isn't an option for most of us anymore, you might as well get creative in the kitchen—RIP pre-baby years, sigh. And if all else fails, there's always bacon.

Pumpkin Holiday-Spiced Granola

Emilia Jamieson

❝ I love making this for my daughter, Ivy, because store-bought granola has so much junk in it. This healthy homemade version is also a great way to get her to eat yogurt and fruit, and you can plate the granola to look really beautiful and interesting for a child. **❞**

MAKES 8 CUPS
PREP TIME: 20 minutes
COOK TIME: 15 to 20 minutes

3 cups old-fashioned oats

½ cup sliced almonds

½ cup chopped walnuts

¼ cup sunflower seeds

¼ cup sesame seeds

¼ cup pumpkin seeds

⅓ cup agave, maple syrup, or honey

½ cup applesauce

¼ cup coconut oil

1 tsp ground cinnamon

½ tsp ground nutmeg

¼ tsp ground cardamom

1 tsp vanilla

½ tsp salt

1½ cups unsweetened shredded coconut

1 cup dried currants or raisins

½ cup dried goji berries

½ cup sliced dried apricots

½ cup sliced pitted dates

Preheat the oven to 350°F. Line a baking sheet with parchment paper.

In a large bowl, combine the oats, nuts, seeds, sweetener of your choice, applesauce, oil, spices, vanilla, and salt and toss to coat.

Transfer to the prepared baking sheet and bake for 15 to 20 minutes, stirring halfway through.

Remove from the oven and place the baking sheet on a cooling rack. Let cool, then add the coconut and dried fruit and mix to combine. Store in an airtight container at room temperature for up to 2 weeks.

Akoté

Marie Fitrion

" I travelled to Haiti with my parents as a teen and fell in love with this little old lady street vendor named Ti-Tante (little aunt). She must have been 95 years old, and she made the most delicious dessert called akoté. It's a sweet, firm cornmeal pudding cut up in squares or served in banana leaves, similar to a tamale. Since that trip I've searched high and low for an akoté recipe only to find out it's a dish very specific to Jacmel, where my family is from. The closest thing I've come across is another Haitian dish called doukounou (which can be made sweet or savoury). This is an adapted recipe and tastes just like the akoté Ti-Tante used to make. It's a simple, delicious dessert, and we like to reduce the sugar a bit and feed it to my daughters, Isobel and Éloïse, as a weekend breakfast alongside fruit and yogurt. "

SERVES 8 TO 10
PREP TIME: 5 minutes + 1 hour cooling
COOK TIME: 5 minutes

1 cup medium cornmeal

¾ to 1 cup sugar, to taste

¼ tsp salt

½ tsp ground cinnamon

¼ tsp ground allspice

2 cups coconut milk

2 cups evaporated milk

1 tbsp coconut oil

1¼ tbsp vanilla

Line an 8-inch square cake pan with parchment paper and place on a cooling rack.

In a medium non-stick saucepan, combine all the ingredients. Bring to a boil, whisking constantly. Lower the heat to a simmer and whisk vigorously for 3 minutes. Pour the mixture into the prepared cake pan and let cool for 1 hour.

Serve warm, gently reheated in the oven or microwave, or cold. Store in an airtight container in the fridge for up to 3 days.

Brown Butter Cinnamon Buns

Katie Shmelinski

❝ I've always loved baking for my family and entertaining people in our home—and the best thing to have while enjoying a cup of coffee with friends is a cinnamon bun. And I've always loved cinnamon buns with cream cheese icing too! I've also never met a kid who doesn't love a cinnamon bun, and these are certainly a favourite of my little ones. Browning the butter adds flavour and transforms the traditional recipe we all know and love into something unique and delicious. Although our spot, The Everyday Kitchen, is primarily a sourdough doughnut shop, on Mondays we serve our brown butter cinnamon buns and a whole bunch of people always show up. **❞**

MAKES 12
PREP TIME: 45 minutes + 2 hours rising
COOK TIME: 25 to 30 minutes

BUNS

2 cups milk

¼ cup plus 2 tbsp butter

4½ tsp instant yeast

2 tbsp sugar

½ tsp salt

4½ cups all-purpose flour,
    plus more if needed

FILLING

½ cup butter, softened

½ cup brown sugar or
    coconut sugar

2 tbsp ground cinnamon

ICING

½ cup butter

½ cup cream cheese

1½ cups icing sugar

MAKE THE BUNS: In a medium saucepan, heat the milk and butter to 110°F. It should be warm to the touch. Do not overheat the milk, as it can kill the yeast. The butter will not be fully melted, which is fine.

Transfer the mixture to a large mixing bowl or the bowl of a stand mixer. Add the yeast and let proof for 10 minutes.

Add the sugar, salt, and flour and mix until the dough comes together. If using a mixer, use the dough hook and mix on medium-low speed until the dough is soft and begins to release from the sides of the mixer, about 5 to 7 minutes. Add some flour by the tablespoon, if needed to reach the desired consistency. If using your hands, transfer the dough to a lightly floured work surface. Knead until the dough is smooth and all the flour is incorporated. Add flour by the tablespoon, again, if needed to reach the desired consistency.

Place in a lightly oiled bowl and let rise, covered, until doubled in size, about 1½ hours.

MAKE THE FILLING: Lightly grease a 9 × 13-inch baking pan. Set aside.

In a small bowl, combine the butter, sugar, and cinnamon. Mix using either your hands or a spoon. I prefer using my hands, since I can finish softening the butter with the heat of my hands. It should be very soft and close to melted so you don't rip the dough when you spread it on.

Place the dough on a lightly floured work surface and dust the top with flour. Using a rolling pin, roll the dough out into a rectangle approximately 11 × 18 inches.

FILL AND BAKE THE BUNS: Top the dough with the filling and, using your hands or a butter knife, gently spread it over the dough's entire surface.

Continued

Roll up the dough width-wise, starting with the longest edge nearest to you. Try to roll it fairly tight. Using a serrated knife, cut the dough in half, then cut each half into six pieces. Place the buns in the prepared baking pan, fairly close together. Cover and let rise for 30 minutes.

Preheat the oven to 350°F. Bake the buns for 25 to 30 minutes, until they are golden brown. Remove from the oven and let cool while you make the icing.

MAKE THE ICING: In a small saucepan over medium heat, melt the butter. We want the butter to brown but not burn. It will begin to bubble, then sizzle, and should be watched closely. Swirl the pan from time to time to check on its colour. Once it stops sizzling, it should be ready. Take the pan off the heat. The butter should be golden brown and smell fragrant.

Transfer the hot butter to the bowl of a stand mixer fitted with the paddle attachment along with the cream cheese and icing sugar. Mix on medium-high speed until the icing is smooth. Top the still-warm buns with the icing and enjoy!

Country Inn Pancakes with Maple Syrup

Michael Smith

66 These hearty and wholesome pancakes are a Saturday morning staple in our home. Making them together is a family ritual, so I've loved watching my kids master them for themselves over time. We even have them on the menu for guests of our family business, The Inn at Bay Fortune. **99**

MAKES 6 TO 8
PREP TIME: 10 minutes
COOK TIME: 20 minutes

1 cup all-purpose flour

1 cup whole wheat flour

1 cup quick oats (not instant)

2 tbsp baking powder

1 tsp ground nutmeg

½ tsp salt

4 eggs

2 cups milk

2 tbsp vegetable oil or melted butter, plus more for pan

1 tsp vanilla

Maple syrup, to serve

Photo on page v

In a large bowl, combine the flours, oats, baking powder, nutmeg, and salt, mixing to combine.

In a medium bowl, whisk together the eggs, milk, oil or butter, and vanilla. Add the wet ingredients to the dry and stir with a wooden spoon—a few quick strokes should do it—until a smooth batter forms.

Heat a large non-stick skillet over medium-low heat. Add a bit of oil or butter to coat the pan. Drop spoonfuls of the batter onto the skillet in any shape you want. Cook until the bottom is golden brown and holes appear on the top. Carefully flip the pancakes and marvel at the gentle rise, promising a fluffy, tender interior. Continue cooking until the underside is golden brown. Repeat with the remaining batter.

The pancakes can be kept warm in a 200°F oven while you cook the remainder. Serve immediately with lots of maple syrup.

Oatmeal Waffles

Tara O'Brady

❝ Waffles and pancakes were the first breakfast dishes I taught my children to cook. With my pair, the wet-versus-dry ingredient division meant each had an equal task to take care of, with just enough busyness to make them feel properly involved in the process. I also appreciated that this early procedural knowledge set them up for success with muffins and quick breads later in their studies.

These waffles are heartier than most, with a generous amount of oats taking the place of the usual flour. Browning the butter and toasting the oats brings a lovely nuttiness to the production, subtly underscored by a whisper of nutmeg. Ground cinnamon, ground ginger, or cardamom would be welcomed as well. Off the iron, the waffles are gratifyingly crunchy, but as they cool, they turn tender, settling into a soft crumb pliant enough to be rolled around a filling and eaten on the go. **❞**

MAKES ABOUT 6
PREP TIME: 10 minutes
COOK TIME: 15 minutes

1 cup all-purpose flour

¼ cup cornstarch

2 tbsp sugar

1 tsp salt

1 tsp baking powder

½ tsp baking soda

¼ tsp ground nutmeg

¼ cup butter, cubed

¾ cup quick oats (not instant) or multigrain hot cereal

1½ cups cold buttermilk or milk

2 eggs

1 tsp vanilla

In a large bowl, whisk together the flour, cornstarch, sugar, salt, baking powder, baking soda, and nutmeg.

Tip the butter into a heavy-bottomed saucepan. Melt over medium heat, then continue to cook, stirring, until the solids begin to brown, about 4 minutes. Stir in the oats and cook for 2 minutes more. Pull from the heat and pour in the buttermilk or milk.

One at a time, whisk the eggs into the oat mixture, followed by the vanilla.

Pour the wet ingredients into the bowl of dry ingredients and whisk to combine. Leave the batter to stand for 5 minutes while the waffle iron heats.

Use the recommended amount of batter for your iron, and cook until the waffles are thoroughly golden and release easily from the pan. Serve immediately or keep warm in a 200°F oven.

Cool any leftover waffles on a baking sheet, then freeze, uncovered, until solid. Transfer to an airtight container and store frozen for up to 1 month. Reheat in a toaster whenever the mood strikes.

NOTE: For the crispiest, airiest waffles, separate the eggs. Add the yolks to the oats as written, and beat the whites on their own to stiff peaks. Gently fold the whites into the batter just before cooking.

Crepes

Cat McInroy

66 Crepes were a favourite of mine growing up. My mother made a Czech version filled with cottage cheese and sweetened with sugar and cinnamon. My children and their friends request crepes every time there's a sleepover. I've had many a phone call from the other moms saying, "Why can't you just do something simple like pancakes or cereal? Now my kids want me to make crepes!" The truth is, crepes are simpler to make than pancakes and take much less time to cook. There is some technique involved in swirling the pan quickly so the thin batter spreads before it cooks, but with a little practice, it becomes quite easy. I teach this to kids and adults alike at the breakfast classes at my cooking school. At home, I set up an assembly line with the young guests where I make the crepes and they dress them with all the fillings they love. Melted butter, sugar or cinnamon sugar, and lemon are our favourite combination by far, though Nutella and strawberries or bananas are a close second. **99**

MAKES 8 TO 12
PREP TIME: 5 minutes
COOK TIME: 15 minutes

1½ cups milk

3 eggs

2 tbsp canola, grapeseed, or
   sunflower oil or melted butter,
   plus more for pan

1 cup all-purpose flour

Melted butter, for serving

Sugar or cinnamon sugar,
   for sprinkling

Place the milk, eggs, and oil in a blender and blend until smooth. Add the flour and blend until the flour is fully incorporated and the batter is smooth. Scrape the sides of the blender to ensure all the flour is well mixed. The consistency should be runny and barely coat the back of a spoon.

Heat a medium frying pan over medium heat. Add a bit of oil to lightly grease the pan. Add just enough batter to cover half of the bottom of the frying pan. Swirl the pan immediately to distribute all the batter over the entire surface of the bottom of the pan. Cook until the crepe starts to pull away from the sides and the bottom is golden brown, about 1 minute. Flip the crepe if you would like both sides browned.

Remove the crepe from the pan, brush with melted butter, and sprinkle sugar or cinnamon sugar over the entire surface. Roll up or fold into quarters and place on your serving plate. Continue with the remaining batter.

Once cooked, any leftover crepes may be stacked between pieces of parchment paper or waxed paper. Store in a zip-lock bag in the fridge for up to 3 days, or frozen for 1 month. Reheat in a frying pan before serving.

NOTE: If your crepe batter seems too thick, whisk in a few tablespoons of milk. If it is too thin, let it sit a few minutes before using. The starch in the flour will thicken the batter as it sits.

Dan Bing

Michelle Jobin

❝ My husband is originally from Taiwan, and it's incredibly important to us that our son understands and appreciates as much about his heritage as possible. Language is a big part of that, as is food, and for us there is nothing that makes us think about Taiwan more than the breakfasts that we've had there. Specifically, dan bing: savoury, crepe-like flatbread that is wrapped around scrambled eggs and topped with soy sauce (I also like it with chili paste, though not so much for the kiddos). It's delicious and filling, and it instantly transports us back to early-morning breakfasts at the little neighbourhood spots in Taipei that we love so much. **❞**

MAKES 12

PREP TIME: 20 minutes
    + 40 minutes resting

COOK TIME: 30 minutes

CREPES

4 cups all-purpose flour

½ cup finely chopped
    green onions

1 tbsp pepper

2 tsp salt

1 cup boiling water

⅓ cup cold water

Canola oil, for work surface

TO SERVE, FOR EACH CREPE

1½ tbsp canola oil

1 egg

Soy sauce

Chinese chili paste (optional)

White pepper

MAKE THE CREPES: In a large bowl, combine the flour, green onions, pepper, and salt and mix. Slowly add the boiling water, mixing with a chopstick or fork. Add the cold water and continue to mix with your hands until the water is completely absorbed into the dough. Cover the dough and let rest for 20 minutes.

Knead the dough again until it is smooth and no longer sticky. Divide the dough into 12 evenly sized balls and let rest for 20 minutes.

Lightly oil a work surface and roll out each ball into a flat, even circle about $\frac{1}{16}$-inch thick. Layer the crepes between pieces of plastic wrap and store them in a zip-lock bag in the fridge for up to 3 days or freeze them for up to 3 months.

TO SERVE: In a medium frying pan over medium heat, heat 1 tablespoon of the oil. Add the crepe (fresh or frozen) to the oil and fry until it is slightly transparent and covered in golden, crispy bubbles. Remove from the pan.

Add the remaining ½ tablespoon oil to the pan. Add the egg, stir, and immediately top with the crepe. Turn the crepe as soon as the egg is cooked and roll it up so the egg is encased inside. Cut into pieces and serve with soy sauce, chili paste, and white pepper. Enjoy!

Uitsmijter

Hidde Zomer

❝ Uitsmijter ("OUT-smy-ter") is a popular Dutch dish consisting of two or three sunny-side-up eggs fried with ham and Dutch Gouda and served open-faced on good dark, buttered bread—though sourdough or ciabatta work well too. It's super easy to make and the ingredients are almost always on hand, at least in a typical Dutch kitchen. Uitsmijter is officially a lunch dish, but for many people it is more commonly enjoyed as a late-night snack after a big night out at the bars. You'd be hard pressed to find a Dutch parent who hasn't been awakened in the middle of the night to the smell of ham and eggs cooking, a sure sign their grown children are back from the club. Directly translated, the Dutch word *uitsmijter* means "bouncer." It's believed that the dish was named after Amsterdam's nightclub doormen, who would typically order this meal in the city's late-night cafés at the end of a long night of managing unruly patrons.

In my house, though, we start the day with it, especially when we have big plans with the kids. Even when prepared in smaller, individual portions, this is a hearty dish that sustains our young boys, and all their "bouncer" energy, through most of the day. They love uitsmijter, and they love helping to make it, especially the part where they get to crack the eggs. ❞

MAKES 4
PREP TIME: 5 minutes
COOK TIME: 8 minutes

4 slices good bread
(like sourdough or whole
wheat with a firm crust)

2 tbsp butter

4 slices cooked ham

4 eggs

4 slices mild Gouda cheese
(any melty cheese will do)

Salt and pepper, to taste

Leafy greens, like arugula
(optional)

Sliced tomatoes (optional)

Butter one side of each slice of bread. Set aside. Melt the remaining butter in a large frying pan over medium-low heat.

When the butter begins to foam, add the sliced ham and cook for a few minutes. Crack an egg on top of each slice of ham and let it cook gently for 2 to 3 minutes. If you like your eggs cooked medium-well, cover the pan with a lid and let the eggs cook to the desired level of doneness.

Once the whites have set, place a slice of cheese on top of each egg and cover the pan. Let the cheese melt for 1 minute, then remove from the heat.

Place the ham and egg on top of the prepared bread and season to taste with salt and pepper. I like to top ours with a little lettuce and tomato to add a little brightness to the dish, but you certainly don't have to! Smakelijk eten!

Savoury Coconut Pancakes

Chanthy Yen

66 Living in Canada as part of an immigrant family from Cambodia, my grandmother and I challenged ourselves with diversifying our pantry, adding a new ingredient each week. One time we took on pancake mix, which was an item we had no clue how to use but that connected us with a fundamental knowledge of flour. This is my adaptation of that first little pancake victory, without all the additives from your boxed varieties. These savoury coconut pancakes are versatile, healthy, and quite easy to make. Use them as a wrap or taco, or eat them as they are for breakfast, lunch, or, better, dinner! These fluffy little clouds are best served as pictured here: add some pulled chicken, a fragrant herb salad, and a sweet tangy sauce. 99

SERVES 4
PREP TIME: 10 minutes
COOK TIME: 20 minutes

1¾ cups all-purpose flour

1 tbsp baking powder

1 tsp baking soda

2 tsp sugar

1 tsp ground turmeric

1 tsp salt

1 (500 ml/16.9 oz) can
    coconut milk

2 eggs

1 tbsp rice wine vinegar

1 cup chopped green onions

In a medium bowl, sift the dry ingredients together. In a separate bowl, combine the coconut milk, eggs, vinegar, and green onions. Add the wet ingredients to the dry and mix until it becomes a smooth batter.

Heat a non-stick skillet over medium heat, and cook the pancakes one at a time: Pour about ¼ cup of pancake batter into the pan and cook until golden brown on both sides, about 2 to 3 minutes in total. Repeat with the remaining batter. Keep the cooked pancakes on a plate covered in foil while you cook the remainder. If there is an extra pancake, it is your responsibility to "taste."

Chicken Souse

Raquel Fox

❝ Unlike any other day of the week, my children look forward to Saturdays. They seem to have some sort of genetically engineered alarm system reserved for waking them up early on this day. The same was true for me as a child, and my grandmother never understood it. Cartoons and chicken souse were a Saturday morning (breakfast or brunch) tradition in the Bahamas where I grew up—enjoying this salutary feel-good type of chicken soup was a catalyst for having a great day. Just hearing my grandmother call "The souse is ready!" triggered a stampede of little bare feet toward the kitchen. Now that my own boys are young men, the kid in all of us still reunites to savour bowls of this comforting lime- and chili-based soup, balanced on TV trays as we watch vintage cartoons. ❞

SERVES 4 TO 6
PREP TIME: 30 minutes
COOK TIME: 35 minutes

2.2 kg (5 lb) boneless, skinless
   chicken thighs, halved or cubed

¼ cup white vinegar

1 tbsp allspice, crushed

1 dry bay leaf

½ large onion, halved and sliced

2 stalks celery, diced

1 tbsp whole allspice berries

1 tsp fresh thyme leaves

Juice of 8 limes

1 tbsp salt

1 whole Scotch bonnet pepper
   (optional)

Hot pepper sauce, to taste

¼ cup chili oil, to garnish

Lime wedges and lime leaves,
   to garnish

Johnnycake (like on page 29)
   or dinner rolls, to serve

Photos on pages 30 to 31

In a large pot, place the chicken and enough water to cover it and bring to a boil.

Add the vinegar, crushed allspice, and bay leaf. Cook for 5 minutes. Remove from the heat and drain the chicken using a colander.

Return the empty pot to the stove and turn the heat to medium-low. Add the onions, celery, allspice berries, thyme, half the lime juice, half the salt, and the pepper. Place the chicken over the vegetables and cover tightly with the lid of the pot. Let the mixture sweat for 10 minutes to develop the flavourful broth.

Add enough water to cover the chicken by 3 inches. Bring to a boil, leaving the lid ajar. Add the remaining lime juice and salt and the pepper sauce. Stir and continue cooking for about 20 minutes more, until the chicken is fully cooked. Taste and adjust the seasoning as needed. Carefully remove the Scotch bonnet pepper before serving.

Serve in bowls garnished with chili oil, lime wedges, and lime leaves, and serve with a slice of johnnycake or dinner rolls to sop up the broth.

Aunt Tia's 18th-Century Johnnycake

Raquel Fox

66 Show me a kid who doesn't appreciate a good pirate's tale and I will show you 10 more who do. It's been over a decade since I started sharing the intriguing origin of johnnycake with my kids, nieces, and nephews. In my best interpretation of a female pirate's voice, I begin, "Ahoy, me hearties! Sit back and I'll tell you a tale of the bread that we're about to eat. It dates back to the 18th century, when the pirates of the Caribbean made this scrumptious bread on the decks of their vessels by building a fire in a box filled with sand to keep the flames from spreading to the craft. It was originally called journey cake because it was quick to make and kept the pirates sustained while travelling. All hand hoy!" 99

SERVES 8
PREP TIME: 15 minutes
COOK TIME: 35 to 40 minutes

2 cups all-purpose flour

1 cup sugar (or ½ cup for
    less-sweet bread)

2 tbsp baking powder

¼ tsp salt

¼ cup butter, cubed

2 tbsp vegetable or canola oil

1 cup milk

¼ cup heavy cream

Photos on pages 30 to 31

Preheat the oven to 350°F. Butter an 8-inch square baking dish.

In a large bowl, combine the flour, sugar, baking powder, and salt and mix to combine. Add the butter, using your hand to break it up into smaller pieces and combine it with the flour.

Add the oil, then slowly add the milk, constantly mixing with one hand until the dough forms a ball. The dough should be soft and pliable.

On a lightly floured work surface, knead the dough a few times. Place the dough in the baking dish and pat it evenly into the dish using your hands.

Pour the cream over the dough and bake until golden and a toothpick inserted into the centre comes out clean, about 35 to 40 minutes.

Serve warm with butter, jam, jelly, or lemon curd, or as a side dish with soups and stews.

Connie & John's Bagels

Connie DeSousa & John Jackson

" This is an amazing bagel recipe that is super kid friendly and easy to make. We love to make it with our little ones! **"**

MAKES 8 BAGELS

**PREP TIME: 20 minutes + 1 hour
10 minutes rising**

COOK TIME: 25 minutes

3 cups bread flour
    (preferably organic)

½ cup whole wheat flour
    (preferably organic)

1 tbsp instant yeast

1 tbsp sugar

1½ tsp salt

320 ml water

1 tbsp molasses

1 egg

¼ cup (total) sesame seeds,
    garlic flakes, pumpkin seeds,
    sunflower seeds, nigella
    seeds, etc.

Coarse sea salt

In a large bowl, combine the flours, yeast, sugar, and salt and mix to combine. Add the water and mix until a dough forms. Transfer the dough to a lightly floured work surface and knead for 10 minutes. Cover with a damp cloth and let rise for 1 hour.

Cut the dough into eight even pieces and shape them into balls. Cover and let rise for 10 minutes.

Shape the bagels by pressing your thumb all the way through the centre of each dough ball. Use your fingers to stretch it out using a rolling motion.

Preheat the oven to 425°F. Lightly oil a baking sheet. Set aside.

Bring a large pot of water to a boil. Add the molasses and stir to dissolve.

Carefully transfer the bagels to the pot of boiling water and boil for 1½ minutes per side. You might have to do this in batches. Transfer the bagels to the prepared baking sheet.

In a small bowl, whisk the egg with 1 teaspoon water. Using a pastry brush, gently brush the tops of the bagels with this egg wash. Sprinkle the bagels with the seeds or other topping and the coarse salt.

Bake for 18 minutes. Let the bagels cool on a cooling rack. Store in an airtight container at room temperature for up to 1 week or slice in half and freeze for up to 1 month.

Soups

I'm not sure about you, but in my house, soups have always been a pretty easy sell. I love them because you can sneak in veggies your kids would otherwise never touch, let alone put in their mouths (thank you, hand mixer), so it makes you feel like you're doing something right when your child slurps up a bowl of nourishing soup, even if it does make a huge mess. Bright orange Cheeto finger stains all over the couch, on the other hand, not so much.

Cream of Tomato Soup

Renée Lavallée

66 Ever since my restaurant The Canteen opened in 2014, my kids have been continuously begging me for this cream of tomato soup, which we serve there with grilled cheese. Both Zoe and Philippe swear by this soup, saying it's the best thing I make! On rainy days at home, you will often find me making a big batch of this soup; half to eat and half to freeze for later when the kids are hungry and want something quick and easy after school. Serve it with Philippe's Crouton Salad (page 70) and you have a quick, nutritious dinner that everyone will love. 99

SERVES 4
PREP TIME: 15 minutes
COOK TIME: 1 hour 20 minutes

½ cup olive oil

1 white onion, cut into large dice

5 cloves garlic, minced

2 dry bay leaves

1 tbsp fennel seeds

1 tsp crushed red pepper flakes (optional)

¼ cup packed brown sugar

2 (796 ml/28 oz) cans San Marzano tomatoes, crushed

2 cups heavy cream

Salt and pepper, to taste

Fresh basil, chopped (optional)

In a large pot over medium heat, heat the oil. Add the onions and garlic and sauté until they are softened but not browned.

Add the bay leaves, fennel seeds, and crushed red pepper flakes. Cook for a few minutes until fragrant. Add the sugar and stir, being careful not to burn the sugar. Cook for 5 minutes.

Add the tomatoes and stir to combine. Lower the heat and simmer for 1 hour, stirring occasionally.

Transfer the soup to a blender and purée until smooth. Place back into the pot and stir in the cream, rewarming the soup if needed. Season to taste with salt and pepper. Top with some basil, if desired. Store in an airtight container in the freezer for up to 3 months.

Carrot Ginger Soup

Rogelio Herrera

66 I wanted to come up with a recipe that's fun and healthy and that can help kids with respiratory problems—my son has asthma. Ginger and turmeric are known to help with inflammation, and carrots are an excellent immune booster, with lots of vitamins and minerals. If it helps them eat the soup, let little ones garnish it with a happy-face design—yogurt for the mouth, some parsley leaves for hair, olive oil for some freckles, and paprika for rosy cheeks. It makes me very happy to think that this soup will be enjoyed by a lot of kids. 99

SERVES 4 TO 6
PREP TIME: 10 minutes
COOK TIME: 40 minutes

2 tbsp olive oil

1.1 kg (2½ lb) organic carrots, peeled and chopped

½ cup chopped yellow onions

1 tbsp ground ginger or ½ tbsp grated fresh ginger

½ tsp ground turmeric

4 cups cold water

2 cups coconut milk

Salt, to taste

1 cup Balkan yogurt, in a squeeze bottle

In a large pot over medium heat, heat the oil. Add the carrots and onions and sauté until soft, about 8 minutes, stirring constantly to prevent scorching.

Add the ginger and turmeric and stir until the carrots are coated with the spices, about 2 minutes.

Add the water and coconut milk, and season with salt to taste. Bring the soup to a boil, then reduce to a simmer and cook for 30 minutes, stirring occasionally.

Remove from the heat and let cool for 10 minutes. Using a blender, purée the soup a few cups at a time until smooth. Pass the purée through a fine-mesh sieve. Taste and adjust the seasoning as needed.

To serve, ladle the soup into bowls and drizzle with the yogurt in the shape of a happy face, if you like. Store in an airtight container in the freezer for up to 3 months.

NOTE: This recipe is vegetarian and gluten-free, and if the yogurt is left out, it's vegan.

Parsnip & Apple Soup

Jeremy Charles

66 My daughter, Iris, loves the fall season. We head to our cabin to go berry picking, and on the way we stop to pick up vegetables along the roadside. Parsnips are one of her favourites. In this recipe, I add a little local honey to sweeten things at the end! 99

SERVES 10 TO 12
PREP TIME: 15 minutes
COOK TIME: 45 minutes

6 tbsp butter

3 cups chopped sweet onions

2 leeks, cleaned and diced

2 fresh bay leaves

Salt, to taste

1.1 kg (2½ lb) parsnips, peeled
   and chopped

4 Fuji apples, peeled, cored,
   and cut into ½-inch cubes
   (you can also use crabapples)

6 cups chicken or vegetable stock

6 cups water

2 cups heavy cream

2 tbsp local honey

2 tbsp apple cider vinegar

Pepper, to taste

In a large pot over medium heat, melt 4 tablespoons of the butter. Add the onions, leeks, bay leaves, and a pinch of salt and cook for 5 to 7 minutes.

Add the parsnips, apples, stock, and water and bring to a boil. Cover and simmer for 30 minutes.

Remove the lid and add the cream, honey, and apple cider vinegar. Continue to cook for 5 minutes, until the parsnips are tender.

Season with salt and pepper. Add the remaining 2 tablespoons of butter and purée with an immersion blender until smooth. Store in an airtight container in the freezer for up to 3 months.

Deccan Dal & Spinach

Joe Thottungal

> For the last 16 years, I have taken Tuesdays off and we have cooked as a family. It makes the kids so happy, and my wife, Suma, is able to take a break from the kitchen and be my guest as we enjoy an amazing homemade meal together. My daughter, Marieann, and my son Michael are all about grilled steak (page 196). They are on the fancier side of the spectrum, but my other son, Mathew, enjoys a simple dal. This one pot meal is all he needs and he's happy.

SERVES 4 TO 6
PREP TIME: 20 minutes
COOK TIME: 25 minutes

3 cups dry red lentils, rinsed
  and drained

6 cups water

1 tbsp + ½ tsp salt

1½ tsp ground turmeric

2 tbsp coconut oil

½ tbsp black mustard seeds

½ tbsp cumin seeds

1 sprig curry leaves

1 cup chopped shallots

8 cloves garlic, chopped

2 green chilies, chopped

½ tsp chili powder

1 cup chopped tomatoes

1 cup chopped spinach

Juice of ½ lime

2 tbsp chopped cilantro

In a large heavy-bottomed pot, bring the lentils and water to a boil. Reduce the heat and add 1 tablespoon of the salt and 1 teaspoon of the turmeric and cook for 10 minutes, stirring occasionally, until the lentils are soft. Set aside.

In a small frying pan, heat the oil over medium-high heat. Add the mustard and cumin seeds and stir until fragrant. Add the curry leaves and cook for 2 minutes. Add the shallots, garlic, and green chilies and cook for 2 minutes. Reduce the heat to low and cook for 2 minutes, stirring occasionally.

Once the shallots are translucent, add the remaining turmeric and the chili powder. Cook for 1 minute. Add the tomatoes and spinach and cook for 2 minutes.

Bring the lentils back to a simmer, add the spinach mixture, and bring to a boil. Season with the remaining salt, the lime juice, and the cilantro. Serve with steamed basmati rice. Store in an airtight container in the freezer for up to 3 months.

Sweet Potato & Coconut Soup

Ralph Alerte Desamours & Lee-Anne Millaire Lafleur

❝ This soup became our kids' favourite for two reasons: First, one of the family outings we love best is going to a farmers' market. We let the kids choose all sorts of veggies, and then Ralph makes something that night with the produce they chose. The second reason is that our oldest son's favourite colour is orange, so one day he decided that he would find orange veggies at the market. He discovered sweet potatoes, and Ralph made soup with them that night. Our son said the colour was too dark, so Ralph added coconut milk to get the best shade of orange possible. The coconut milk also made the soup a little sweeter, and turned it into an instant favourite for all three of our boys. ❞

SERVES 4 TO 6

PREP TIME: 10 minutes

COOK TIME: 20 minutes

16 cups water

6 sweet potatoes, peeled
    and cubed

4 carrots, peeled and chopped

1 onion, peeled and chopped

½ leek, chopped

2 cups coconut milk

½ cup sugar, honey, or agave

¼ cup butter or vegan butter

3 tbsp grated fresh ginger

1 tbsp ground coriander

Salt and pepper, to taste

In a large pot, combine all of the ingredients and bring to a boil. Lower the heat and simmer for 20 minutes. Using an immersion blender, purée the soup until it is very smooth. Season with salt and pepper to taste. Store in an airtight container in the freezer for up to 3 months.

Chicken & Lime Soup

Cat McInroy

" I discovered chicken and lime soup in Mexico when I was pregnant with our son. My stomach was a bit queasy, and the soup settled it, which made that holiday immensely better. This recipe is now the go-to for my family when we're feeling under the weather. Its flavourful broth is marvellously restorative, just as a great broth should be. I teach this recipe in the "Preparing to Launch" youth/young adult classes at my cooking school in Whitehorse, Yukon Territory; it's very easy to make, extremely budget-friendly, only takes one pot (which makes it perfect for college students), and the leftovers freeze well. It's the new favourite of every person who tries it. **"**

SERVES 4 TO 6
PREP TIME: 30 minutes
COOK TIME: 30 minutes

1 tbsp olive oil

1 medium yellow or white onion, cut into small dice

2 stalks celery, cut into small dice

3 to 4 cloves garlic, minced

1 medium jalapeño, seeds and veins removed to keep the spice milder, minced (optional)

1½ tsp dried oregano

1¾ tsp ground cumin

2 tsp salt, or more to taste

½ tsp pepper

1 (355 ml/12 oz) can diced tomatoes with chilies (see Note)

6 to 8 cups low-sodium chicken broth (I like lots of broth, so I use the larger amount)

1 to 2 limes

1 large chicken breast (bone-in, skin-on gives best flavour)

1 bunch cilantro, rinsed, drained, and roughly chopped

1 to 2 medium avocados, cubed, to garnish (optional)

Tortilla chips, to serve

In a medium pot, heat the oil over medium heat. Add the onions and celery and sauté for about 5 minutes, until the vegetables begin to soften. Add the garlic and jalapeño. (Do not brown or sauté the jalapeño on high heat, as you will quite literally "pepper-spray" yourself right out of the kitchen. If you notice yourself starting to cough or have difficulty breathing, it means you're cooking the jalapeño on too high heat.)

Add the oregano, cumin, salt, and pepper. Add the canned tomatoes, broth, juice of 1 lime, and the chicken breast. Stir to combine. Bring the soup to a boil, then reduce to a simmer and cook, covered, for 20 minutes or until the chicken is cooked through.

Remove the chicken from the soup and place on a plate to cool slightly. Using two forks, shred the chicken (removing the skin and bones and discarding them into the compost) and return it to the pot with any juices that may have escaped.

Taste and adjust the seasoning as needed. If you want more zing, add more lime juice. I use at least 1½ limes when I make this soup. It should be flavourful but not unpleasantly limey. At this point, the soup will keep in an airtight container in the fridge for up to 1 week, or the freezer for up to 3 months.

Add half of the cilantro to the soup, keeping the other half for garnish. Omit the cilantro if it isn't your thing, or load it on if it is.

Serve topped with avocado, and with tortilla chips on the side—they are brilliant for scooping up the pieces from the bowl and add a salty punch to the broth—or crumbled on top of the soup.

NOTE: If you can't find canned tomatoes with chilies, you may substitute a small can of chopped tomatoes and a small can of chopped green chilies. Chopped green chilies are not the same as chopped jalapeño peppers—usually a green chili like Anaheim or poblano, which is not as spicy, is used in canned green chilies. You will find the canned green chilies in the Mexican food section or with the taco kits and jarred salsas at your grocery store.

Chicken Noodle Soup

David Gunawan

> ❝ It's good practice to teach our little ones to be grateful for what we have and to extend the resources that are available to us by not wasting food. This recipe does just that by using a whole roasted chicken, meat and bones. ❞

SERVES 4 TO 6

PREP TIME: 20 minutes
+ 10 minutes chilling

COOK TIME: 2¼ hours

STOCK

1 tbsp olive oil

1 medium carrot, coarsely chopped

1 stalk celery, coarsely chopped

½ medium yellow onion, coarsely chopped

1 whole roasted chicken, meat removed, shredded, and reserved for the soup (see Note)

2 sprigs thyme

½ tsp black peppercorns

12 cups water

SOUP

2 medium carrots, cut into medium dice

2 stalks celery, cut into medium dice

½ yellow onion, cut into medium dice

1 tsp minced thyme leaves

1 tsp salt, plus more to taste

Pepper, to taste

1 cup dried egg noodles or whatever noodles you have on hand, broken into bite-sized pieces

Cooked, shredded chicken (see Stock, above, and Note)

MAKE THE STOCK: In a large pot over medium-high heat, heat the oil. Add the vegetables, sautéing until they are translucent. Add the cooked chicken carcass (reserving the meat for later in the recipe), thyme, peppercorns, and water, scraping the bottom of the pot with a wooden spoon to dislodge any browned bits.

Bring the stock to a boil, reduce the heat to a simmer, and let cook for 1½ hours, uncovered. Skim the stock as needed. Remove any large pieces of carcass and discard. Strain the stock through a fine-mesh sieve.

Let cool to room temperature, then chill in the fridge for at least 10 minutes. The stock will keep in an airtight container in the fridge for 3 days or in the freezer for up to 1 month.

MAKE THE SOUP: Place the stock in a medium pot and heat over medium-high heat. Add the carrots, celery, onions, thyme, salt, and pepper. Reduce to a simmer and cook until the vegetables are tender, about 20 minutes.

Meanwhile, bring a large pot of salted water to a boil. Add the noodles and cook according to the package instructions until al dente. Drain the noodles and add them to the soup. Add the shredded cooked chicken and let the soup simmer until the flavours meld, about 5 minutes. Taste and adjust the seasoning as needed and serve. Store leftovers in an airtight container in the freezer for up to 3 months.

NOTE: Depending on how much chicken you like in your soup, you can either use the meat from a whole chicken for this recipe, or make (or buy) a roast chicken for dinner and use the leftovers here (carcass included).

Matzo Ball Soup

Amy Rosen

❝ I've got six nieces and nephews ranging from 8 to 23 years old, and when it comes to big family gatherings, of which there are many, the one dish that the kids and adults agree on is chicken soup with matzo balls. It's a Jewish thing. It's a soulful thing. It's warming and delicious and a must at every holiday. It's basically a meal in a bowl, even though 10 other dishes usually follow the soup course. (That's also a Jewish thing.) The younger kids are often full after the matzo ball soup, so they can just run around, and that's fine because you know they've been fed a semi-balanced meal. My 16-year-old niece Julia has gotten so good at making matzo balls that it has become her job at Passover. Helping kids learn to make things they love is one of the best gifts you can give them. ❞

SERVES 8

PREP TIME: 30 minutes + 1 hour chilling

COOK TIME: 2½ hours

SOUP

1 small whole chicken, trimmed

12 to 14 cups water

3 large carrots, peeled and trimmed

2 stalks celery

2 large yellow onions, halved

1 tbsp salt, plus more to taste

Pepper, to taste

1 small bunch flat-leaf parsley

¼ cup chopped fresh dill + extra to garnish

MATZO BALLS

4 eggs, beaten

1 cup matzo meal

2 tbsp vegetable oil

2 tsp sea salt

¼ tsp pepper

1 tsp baking powder

¼ cup soda water

MAKE THE SOUP: Place the chicken in a large pot and cover with the water. Bring to a boil, uncovered, and skim off any foam that accumulates. Reduce to a simmer. Add the carrots, celery, onions, salt, and pepper. Cook for at least 2 hours, skimming as needed. Add the parsley and dill during the last 10 minutes of cooking.

MEANWHILE, MAKE THE MATZO BALLS: In a large bowl, stir together the eggs, matzo meal, oil, salt, pepper, and baking powder. Fold in the soda water using a spatula. Cover with plastic wrap and refrigerate for 1 hour.

Bring a large pot of salted water to a boil, then lower to a simmer. Using lightly oiled hands, gently shape the matzo mixture into golf-ball-sized balls, placing them in the pot of water as you go. Poach them in the simmering water, covered, until they are soft and cooked through, about 35 to 40 minutes. Remove the matzo balls from the water.

Remove the chicken and vegetables from the broth. Shred or slice the chicken meat. Coarsely chop the carrots, discarding the remaining vegetables and herbs. Strain the broth into a clean pot, using a fine-mesh sieve or a colander lined with cheesecloth.

Taste and adjust the seasoning as needed. Ladle the broth into bowls and add a few pieces of chicken and carrot, and the matzo balls. Garnish with dill. Store the soup and matzo in separate airtight containers in the freezer for up to 3 months.

Pea Soup with Duck Meatballs

Vincent Dion Lavallée

" This is my daughter's favourite soup. I've added the pork and duck meatballs to make it more of a meal, but you can easily leave them out. "

SERVES 8 TO 10

PREP TIME: 45 minutes + 24 hours soaking

COOK TIME: 3 hours

SOUP

6 cups yellow split peas, soaked in water for 24 hours and drained

10 cups chicken stock

1 cup medium-diced onions

1 cup medium-diced carrots

1 cup medium-diced celeriac

2 cloves garlic, minced

200 g (7 oz) smoked pork belly (unsliced)

MEATBALLS

250 g (0.55 lb) ground pork (fatty)

250 g (0.55 lb) ground duck

½ cup dried breadcrumbs

3 cloves garlic, minced

2 tbsp salt

¼ cup heavy cream

1 large egg

1 cup maple syrup

TO SERVE

Olive oil

2-year-old cheddar, shredded

MAKE THE SOUP: Place the drained split peas in a large pot. Add the stock, vegetables, garlic, and pork belly. Bring to a boil then reduce to a simmer and cook over medium heat for 3 hours. The soup is ready when the peas are completely soft and the soup is homogeneous. Remove the pork belly, let cool, and cut into small dice. Set aside for serving.

MEANWHILE, MAKE THE MEATBALLS: Preheat the oven to 400°F and line a baking sheet with parchment paper. In the bowl of a stand mixer fitted with the paddle attachment, combine the pork, duck, breadcrumbs, garlic, salt, cream, and egg. Mix on low speed until the mixture is homogeneous. Shape into golf-ball-sized meatballs and place on the prepared baking sheet. Bake for 10 minutes.

In a medium skillet, over medium-high heat, bring the maple syrup to a boil and let it reduce by half. Add the meatballs and toss to coat them in the syrup.

TO SERVE: Serve the soup piping hot with a drizzle of olive oil, a sprinkling of cheddar, topped with some cubes of the reserved pork belly, and a few maple-glazed meatballs. Store the soup and meatballs in separate airtight containers in the freezer for up to 3 months.

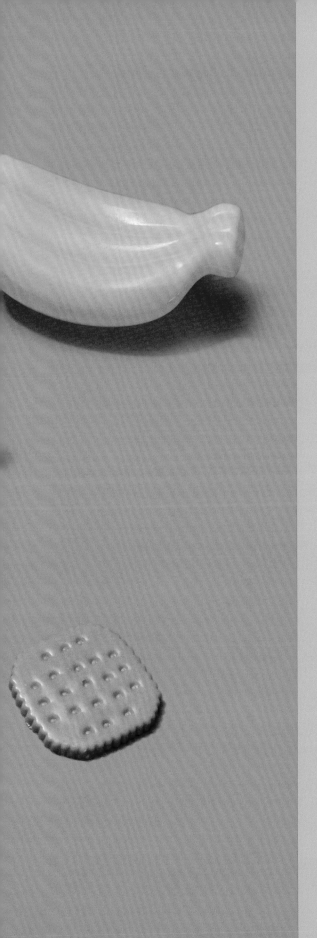

Snacks & Sides

If there's anything I've learned in the process of putting this cookbook together, it's never say never. Like your child eating a side of salad. I know, I know; for a lot of kids, especially the younger ones, a salad is a hard feat to pull off. If yours do eat salad, well done! For my son, I feel like iceberg lettuce and ranch dressing might be something that I aspire to one day. But children have a knack for pulling a full 180 on you and demolishing something you could have never imagined they liked. Chances are they'll roll their eyes and tell you that it's their favourite meal at daycare, like you're totally clueless and they know everything. Get used to it. This chapter is full of fun ideas to try with your kiddos, and who knows, maybe you'll happy-cry watching what they eat with disbelief.

Hummus

Dan Geltner

66 My mom would serve me this classic Israeli-style hummus inside a branch of celery, topped with olives (she used the green ones stuffed with pimento). It was her Middle Eastern version of "ants on a log". **99**

SERVES 6 TO 8
PREP TIME: 20 minutes + overnight soaking
COOK TIME: 1 to 2 hours

4 cups dried chickpeas

3 tsp baking soda

1 medium carrot

½ white onion

2 dry bay leaves

2 cups tahini

1¼ cups lemon juice

1 head roasted garlic, peeled

1 tsp cumin seeds, toasted and ground

Salt, to taste

Good olive oil and pita, or various vegetables, sliced, to serve

Place the chickpeas in a large pot, add 1 teaspoon of the baking soda, and enough cold water to cover the chickpeas by a few inches. Set aside to soak overnight.

Drain the chickpeas and place back in the pot with another teaspoon of the baking soda and enough cold water to cover. Bring to a boil, then remove from the heat and drain. Peel the chickpeas and place them back in the pot. (This step is optional, but it will produce the smoothest hummus ever and is a good job for tiny fingers.)

Cover the chickpeas with cold water, then add the remaining teaspoon of baking soda and the carrot, onion, and bay leaves. Cook until the chickpeas are very soft but not mushy. Cooking time will depend on your chickpeas. Drain and reserve some cooking liquid, discarding the bay leaves.

Place the chickpeas, carrot, and onion in a blender. Add the tahini, lemon juice, garlic, cumin, and a little salt. Purée until smooth, adding some cooking liquid, if needed for consistency. Season with more salt if needed, to taste. Serve with lots of good olive oil on top and good pita, or a bunch of vegetables to dip. Or try it in a celery stick with olives! Hummus will keep for up to 1 week in an airtight container in the fridge.

Dilly Cherry Tomato Fridge Pickles

Camilla Wynne

❝ If there's anything the children I know seem to universally love, it's pickles and cherry tomatoes, so combining the two is a home run. As a toddler, my niece Sophie adorably referred to one of her favourite foods, cherry tomatoes, as "teemos." Now as a sophisticated 10-year-old, she never forgets to subtly remind me how much she enjoys the pickled version I make, in hopes of obtaining another jar. So this one's for Sophie, as well as my childhood self, who loved pickles so much that I would straight-up drink the brine. **❞**

MAKES 2 CUPS
PREP TIME: 10 minutes
  + 24 hours chilling
COOK TIME: 5 to 10 minutes

2 cups cherry tomatoes,
   preferably multicoloured

1 to 2 cloves garlic

2 heads dill

¼ tsp black peppercorns

½ cup + 2 tbsp water

½ cup white vinegar

1½ tsp salt

½ tsp sugar

Wash the cherry tomatoes and pierce each one three to four times, either with a toothpick or the tip of a paring knife.

In a scrupulously clean 16-ounce jar, place the garlic, dill, and peppercorns. Gently but assertively pack in all the tomatoes.

In a small pot, combine the water, vinegar, salt, and sugar. Bring to a boil, stirring to dissolve the salt and sugar. Remove from the heat and let cool for 5 minutes, then pour over the tomatoes to cover. Close the jar tightly and place in the fridge for at least 24 hours before eating. Store in the jar in the fridge for up to 1 month.

Artichauts à la Vinaigrette

J-C Poirier

66 Artichokes are not an easy vegetable for kids—they're definitely outside the box. My mom used to make this simple boiled artichoke vinaigrette dish that makes for a great starter, or you can eat it as part of a picnic on the beach. As a kid, I remember how fun it was to go through all the leaves one by one, dipping them in the vinaigrette and pulling the small amount of meat with my teeth. Then, the big payoff: the artichoke heart is something special. Now I prepare this dish for my daughters, and they love it—maybe not for the artichoke flavour but more for the concept of the dish that shows that eating can be a lot of fun. **99**

SERVES 4
PREP TIME: 15 minutes
COOK TIME: 20 to 30 minutes

4 large globe artichokes, stems
   snapped off

VINAIGRETTE
2 tbsp + 1 tsp sherry vinegar,
   plus more if needed

1 tbsp warm water

1 tsp salt

1 large shallot, minced and soaked
   in cold water, then drained

1½ tsp Dijon mustard

1½ tsp whole-grain mustard

1½ tsp honey

1 clove garlic, finely grated

½ cup olive oil

½ cup grapeseed oil

2 sprigs thyme

1 large pinch pepper

COOK THE ARTICHOKES: Bring a medium pot of salted water to a boil. Add the artichokes and reduce to a simmer. Cook for 20 to 30 minutes. Check for doneness by removing a leaf from the artichoke. If it comes out easily, they are done. Remove the pot from the heat and let the artichokes cool in the water. Remove them from the water and let drain for a few minutes.

MAKE THE VINAIGRETTE: In a medium bowl, whisk together the vinegar, water, and salt until dissolved. Add the shallots, both mustards, honey, and garlic. Mix well. Combine both oils and add to the bowl in a slow, steady stream, whisking all the while. Add the thyme and pepper. Taste and adjust the seasoning as needed.

Serve the vinaigrette alongside the artichokes, dipping each leaf before eating.

Cucumber & Yogurt Salad

Maha Barsoom

❝ This simple side salad is always my favourite on a hot summer day. It's easy, delicious, and a recipe that my mom used to make for us when we were kids, so I grew up loving it. I make it for my own kids all the time because it's also very healthy, and can be thrown together in a flash! Serve it with bread, or alongside any meat or vegetable dish you like. **❞**

SERVES 4

PREP TIME: 10 minutes

1 cup whole-milk plain yogurt
   (3.25%)

¾ cup sour cream or labneh (14%)

2 cloves garlic, minced

1 tsp dried mint

1 large English cucumber or
   5 small cucumbers, diced

Sea salt, to taste

1 sprig mint, to garnish

In a medium bowl, whisk together the yogurt, sour cream or labneh, garlic, and dried mint. Add the diced cucumbers and mix well. Season with sea salt to taste. Top with mint and serve. Store in an airtight container in the fridge for up to 1 week.

Jicama & Carrot Salad

Sandra Soto

66 As little kids in Mexico City, this was the kind of snack we would get from a fresh fruit stand to eat at school. Fresh fruit is a big part of the Mexican diet, and this salad hits all the right notes: spicy, acidic, and refreshing. Serve it alone as a snack, or as a side to almost any dish, especially on a hot day. **99**

SERVES 4 TO 6
PREP TIME: 10 minutes

1 large jicama, julienned

3 medium carrots, grated

2 oranges, cut into segments

Juice of ½ lime

1 tbsp Tajin spice

In a large bowl, combine all the ingredients and toss to combine. Serve.

Mandoline Vegetable Salad

David McMillan

" This is a bit of an "anything goes" salad in terms of ingredients. I like to make it with what I have on my farm at the peak of our summer season, especially if my daughters go and grab the vegetables themselves. Serve it alongside my Pork Schnitzel (page 176). "

SERVES 4 TO 6

PREP TIME: 15 minutes

3 carrots (yellow, red, and orange), peeled

1 white turnip, peeled

1 small celeriac, peeled

1 parsnip, peeled

1 cucumber, peeled

1 small kohlrabi, peeled

1 savoy cabbage heart

½ Vidalia onion

1 apple

DRESSING

3 tbsp apple cider vinegar

2 tbsp honey

2 tsp mustard

¼ cup heavy cream, or more to taste

1 tbsp chopped fresh tarragon

1 tbsp chopped fresh mint

Salt and pepper, to taste

Toasted sunflower seeds, to garnish

Thinly slice the vegetables and apple using a mandoline and place in a large serving bowl.

In a small bowl, whisk together the vinegar, honey, mustard, cream, and herbs, and season with salt and pepper to taste. Pour over the salad, toss to coat, and sprinkle with the sunflower seeds. Serve alongside schnitzel (page 176).

Cauliflower Salad

Caroline Dumas

❝ This is my take on a Middle Eastern roasted cauliflower recipe, but faster and easier to prepare. By adding chickpeas, it gives the dish texture and protein, and the olives and candied lemon give it a complexity and character my daughters love. Serve it with lamb, chicken, or fish, or as a vegetarian main. **❞**

SERVES 4
PREP TIME: 15 minutes
COOK TIME: 12 minutes

1 head cauliflower, cut into florets

1 cup canned chickpeas, rinsed and drained

1 tsp ground cumin

1 tsp ground sumac

Salt, to taste

¼ cup Moroccan olives

½ preserved lemon, thinly sliced

½ fresh red chili, seeded and minced

1 cup coarsely chopped flat-leaf parsley

Juice of 1 lemon

150 g (5 oz) feta or grilled halloumi

Preheat the oven to 425°F. Line a baking sheet with parchment paper.

Bring a medium pot of salted water to a boil and blanch the cauliflower for 2 minutes. Drain.

In a large bowl, combine the cauliflower, chickpeas, spices, and salt to taste. Toss to combine. Transfer to the prepared baking sheet, add the olives, and roast for 10 minutes.

Transfer the cauliflower mixture to a platter and sprinkle with the preserved lemons, chilies, parsley, and lemon juice. Top with the feta or halloumi, and serve. Store in an airtight container in the fridge for up to 3 days.

Crouton Salad

Renée Lavallée

" My son, Philippe, loves three things: cheese, bread, and garlic. This quick and easy salad is a Phil favourite, and he named it Crouton Salad because of the salty and crunchy croutons we make for it. This weeknight go-to pairs perfectly with my Cream of Tomato Soup (page 36) or a bowl of pasta. It's also great to pack into kids' lunches the next day. Both of my kids love helping out when we make it, and I often make extra croutons for them to snack on while waiting for supper to be ready. I should also mention that this salad is not for the faint of heart. There's lots of garlic, which my kids love!. "

SERVES 4
PREP TIME: 15 minutes
COOK TIME: 5 to 10 minutes

CROUTONS

½ baguette, torn into bite-sized pieces

¼ cup olive oil

Salt and pepper, to taste

DRESSING

5 cloves garlic, finely grated

Juice of 2 lemons

½ cup canola oil

½ cup olive oil

½ tbsp Worcestershire sauce

1 tsp crushed red pepper flakes (optional)

1 bunch kale, stems removed and leaves roughly torn

1 cup grated Parmesan

Preheat the oven to 400°F and line a baking sheet with parchment paper.

MAKE THE CROUTONS: In a medium bowl, combine the bread, oil, salt, and pepper and toss to combine. Place on the prepared baking sheet and bake for 5 to 10 minutes, until browned and crispy. Let cool.

MAKE THE DRESSING: In a large bowl, whisk together the dressing ingredients until combined. Add the kale and massage the leaves in the dressing for a minute or two.

Add the croutons and cheese, toss, and season to taste.

Zucchini Bread

Molly Superfine-Rivera & Mehdi Brunet-Benkritly

" I'm somewhat addicted to baked goods, so I like to always have something homemade on the kitchen counter, ready to be picked at. Ideally something that can last all week without needing any special storage or attention. My son, Leon, seems to have inherited this love for cakes and such, so having something healthy and nutritious is imperative. This recipe is simple enough to whip up on a whim and hits all the "healthy" marks: maple instead of sugar (and not too much of it), whole wheat flour, vegetables! Everyone in my house loves it, even the pup, who licks up the crumbs. —Molly **"**

MAKES 1 LOAF
PREP TIME: 10 minutes
COOK TIME: 55 to 60 minutes

2 cups coarsely grated zucchini

2 eggs

1 cup maple syrup

½ cup neutral oil
   (preferably grapeseed)

1 tsp vanilla

1 tsp salt

1 tsp ground cinnamon

⅛ tsp ground nutmeg

¾ tsp baking soda

½ tsp baking powder

1 cup whole wheat flour
   (preferably organic)

1 cup all-purpose flour
   (preferably organic)

Preheat the oven to 350°F. Lightly oil and flour a loaf pan. Set aside.

In a large bowl, combine the zucchini, eggs, maple syrup, oil, vanilla, and salt. Using a fork, mix until combined. Add the spices, baking soda, and baking powder and mix until combined. Add both flours and mix until just combined. Do not overmix.

Transfer the batter to the loaf pan and bake for 55 to 60 minutes, or until a toothpick inserted in the centre of the bread comes out clean. Let cool completely before slicing.

Store the bread, covered, in the loaf pan at room temperature for up to 3 days.

Cornbread

Lisa Ahier

66 Cornbread was a five-star, kid-approved staple in our house when I was growing up. Mom would serve it for breakfast with honey butter; for lunch with pinto beans, onions, and cheddar; and sometimes at dinnertime as a dessert topped with strawberries and whipped cream. She'd cut leftover cornbread into croutons and toss them in salads. If there was still any left after that, she would freeze it and use it to make stuffing for Sunday night's roast chicken dinner. Winner winner chicken dinner, right? But double winner winner chicken dinner when more cornbread is served on the side. 99

MAKES 2 MEDIUM CORNBREADS
PREP TIME: 30 minutes
COOK TIME: 40 minutes

4½ cups all-purpose flour

2 cups sugar

1½ cups coarse-ground cornmeal

4 tsp baking soda

4 tsp salt

9 eggs

2½ cups buttermilk

1½ cups canola oil, plus more to
    oil skillets

1 tsp vanilla

2 cups fresh or frozen corn kernels

Preheat the oven to 400°F. Heat two 6- to 8-inch cast-iron skillets in the oven for 20 minutes.

Place the flour, sugar, cormeal, baking soda, and salt in a large bowl and whisk to combine. Place the the eggs, buttermilk, oil, and vanilla in a medium bowl and whisk until frothy.

Slowly fold the wet ingredients into the dry ingredients. There will be lumps. Stop stirring once all the dry ingredients are incorporated. Fold in the corn kernels.

Using oven mitts, remove the cast-iron skillets from the oven. Add a few teaspoons of oil to each skillet and tilt to evenly coat. Add the batter to the skillets, making sure they are only three-quarters full.

Place the skillets in the oven and bake for 25 minutes. Reduce the oven temperature to 325°F and continue baking another for 15 minutes. A toothpick inserted into the centre should come out clean. Transfer the skillets to a cooling rack and let cool for at least 20 minutes. Cut and serve. Store in an airtight container in the freezer for up to 1 month.

NOTE: This is such an easy recipe to make, and the kids can help. Just be aware of the smoking-hot cast-iron pan going in and out of the oven.

Brother Juniper's Cornbread

Anthony Rose

" This is my version of a recipe from master baker Peter Reinhart, the founder of the award-winning Brother Juniper's Bakery in Santa Rosa, California and author of *Brother Juniper's Bread Book*. This family recipe is super delicious and just fun to make. I use this as a base for not only cornbread but also pancakes, hushpuppies, muffins, and corn dog batter—I love it so much. **"**

MAKES 1 LARGE CORNBREAD
PREP TIME: 20 minutes
COOK TIME: 1 hour

2 cups all-purpose flour

¾ cup medium-ground cornmeal

¾ cup grits

½ cup + 1 tbsp sugar

2 tbsp baking powder

2 tsp salt

1 cup shredded cheddar

1 jalapeño, seeded and minced

2½ cups buttermilk

2 eggs

¼ cup butter, melted

¼ cup olive oil or butter

Preheat the oven to 350°F. Place a 12-inch cast-iron skillet in the oven to heat.

In a large bowl, combine the flour, cornmeal, grits, sugar, baking powder, salt, cheddar, and jalapeño and stir to combine.

In another bowl, combine the buttermilk, eggs, and melted butter and whisk to combine. Add the wet ingredients to the dry ingredients and mix gently by hand.

Carefully remove the now-hot skillet from the oven. Add the oil or butter to the pan and swirl to coat the bottom and sides. Pour the batter into the pan and return it to the oven.

Bake for 1 hour, turning the pan halfway through the cooking time. The cornbread is done when a toothpick inserted into the centre comes out clean. Let cool for a few minutes before unmoulding onto a cooling rack to cool completely. Serve with maple syrup and loads of butter. Store in an airtight container in the fridge for up to 1 week, or in the freezer for up to 3 months.

Golu Molu

Aman Dosanj

> When I was a kid, my granny would welcome me home from school with a freshly made, warm, soft roti, rolled up, and wrapped at the bottom with a paper towel. It was a snack that never interfered with the more important things in life, like playtime. Now my family do the same with my niece. Even though Indian food (like most) is regional, this bread is found in homes across the country—from the north all the way down to the south—so breaking bread is a real thing. Smother it with butter, roll it up, and keep on playing.

MAKES 4 ROTIS
PREP TIME: 15 minutes
COOK TIME: 15 minutes

2 cups whole wheat flour (like Anita's Organic), plus more for rolling (or you can use a mix of 1½ cups all-purpose flour and ½ cup red Fife or other heritage grain)

200 ml lukewarm water

Vegetable oil, if needed

Salted cultured butter or good-quality salted butter, as needed

Place the flour in a medium bowl and make a well. Add the water to the centre of the well and mix until the dough comes together. Knead until smooth, about 2 minutes. You might need to add a drizzle of oil if the dough is too sticky. Cover and let rest for 5 minutes.

Heat a medium skillet over medium-high heat. Divide the dough into four equal pieces. Shape into balls and roll them out with a rolling pin, dusting with flour if needed to prevent sticking. Roll out until they are as thin as possible. Remove any excess flour.

Place a roti in the skillet and cook until it begins to turn brown, about 1 minute. Flip over and cook until the dough is bubbled and browned, then flip again and cook for another minute. Using a clean towel, press on the edges of the bread to help distribute the air and cook the sides, being careful not to burn your hand. It should puff up like a big science experiment.

Once it is cooked, smack the roti to remove the air, then smother it with a pat of butter and roll it up. Cook the remaining roti, removing any excess flour from the pan before adding the next one. Wrap the rotis in foil to keep warm.

Scotch Egg

Aman Dosanj

❛❛ My granny was my person. When I was growing up in England, she lived with us. I've always had this overactive imagination, and teddy-bear picnics were our thing. We would race up and down our long hallway, working up an appetite before our picnic, to which all of my teddy friends were invited. Sausage rolls, cucumber sandwiches, cakes, pastries, and doughnuts were staples. But the humble Scotch egg was the star. It's got to be one of Britain's all-time picnic foods, and for me it's the ultimate finger food: it's round and there's meat and a gooey egg, but it's also crispy crunchy as you bite into it. I like to add a little Indian vibe by shaping spiced kebab mince around the cooked egg instead of the standard pork sausage meat. It's a whole load of British and a tad Indian, just like me. These Scotch eggs have made appearances at my Okanagan Valley pop-up dinners throughout the years (where I live now), but most importantly, they're always present at teddy-bear picnics with my niece, Sianna. ❝❝

MAKES 4 EGGS
PREP TIME: 30 minutes
COOK TIME: 10 minutes

SCOTCH EGGS

4 medium free-range eggs

1 tbsp white vinegar

225 g (½ lb) ground lamb or beef (preferably organic and ethically raised)

1½ tsp minced garlic

1½ tsp minced fresh ginger

1 tsp salt, plus more to taste

1 tsp garam masala

¼ tsp ground Kashmiri chili

1 cup all-purpose flour

2 eggs, whisked

1½ cups dried breadcrumbs (homemade, if possible)

Vegetable oil, for frying

Tomato chutney, to serve (optional)

APPLE RAITA

1 cup yogurt

1 cup grated apple

Toasted and ground cumin seeds, to taste

Salt, to taste

MAKE THE SCOTCH EGGS: Bring a medium pot of salted water to a boil. Carefully lower the eggs into the boiling water and cook for 6 minutes. Remove the eggs from the water, place in an ice bath with the vinegar, and let cool. This will make the eggs easier to peel. Once cooled, carefully peel the eggs and set aside. They will be fragile.

In a medium bowl, combine the ground meat with the garlic, ginger, salt, garam masala, and Kashmiri chili. Mix to combine. Cook a small patty of the meat mixture to taste for seasoning. Adjust the salt and spices as needed.

On a clean work surface, place a sheet of plastic wrap followed by the meat mixture. Top with another sheet of plastic wrap and roll it out until it is about ½-inch thick. Peel back the top layer of plastic wrap. Carefully wrap the eggs with the meat mixture, making sure each egg is fully coated.

Place the flour in a shallow plate. Place the whisked eggs in a small bowl. Place the breadcrumbs in a shallow plate. One by one, dip the eggs in the flour, then in the whisked eggs, and finally in the breadcrumbs.

Heat the oil (deep enough to cover at least half of the egg) in a deep fryer or deep skillet to 360°F. Fry the Scotch eggs until golden brown, turning occasionally, about 5 minutes. Drain the eggs on a paper-towel-lined plate.

MEANWHILE, MAKE THE APPLE RAITA: In a medium bowl, mix all the ingredients together well to combine.

To serve, cut each egg in half, season with a pinch of salt and pepper, and top with the apple raita, or some tomato chutney, if you prefer. Happy eating.

Lloydie's Chicken Wings

Lloyd Tull

❝ The Tull family has a bunch of traditions, most of which don't make sense, and one is around our collective love for chicken wings. Anytime there is a family gathering, the weeks prior are filled with aunts, uncles, cousins, and parents asking me, "Will you be serving chicken wings for Christmas/Passover/Grandma's birthday?" The funny part is that it started as a dish only served on the kids' table, yet somehow, miraculously, all the adults would also end up with a few wings on their plate. What started off as a comfort food for my children has quickly spread to become a family favourite expected at all holidays, family functions, and anytime we can find an excuse to eat together. ❞

MAKES ABOUT 30 WINGS

PREP TIME: 30 minutes + 45 minutes to 24 hours marinating

COOK TIME: 30 to 50 minutes

8 cups water

⅓ cup lemon juice

⅓ cup white vinegar

2 kg (4.4 lb) chicken wings

SEASONING

Salt, to taste

Pepper, to taste

Garlic powder, to taste

4 tsp canola oil

SAUCE

2 cups Kraft BBQ sauce

1 tbsp soy sauce

1 tsp pepper

1 tsp garlic powder,
    or more if desired

Canola oil, for frying

In a large bowl, combine the water, lemon juice, and vinegar. Add the wings and marinate for 15 minutes. Drain the wings in a colander, discarding the water.

MAKE THE SEASONING: In a large bowl, combine the salt, pepper, garlic powder, and oil. Add the wings and let marinate in the fridge for at least 30 minutes, or longer for best results, up to 24 hours.

MEANWHILE, MAKE THE SAUCE: In a medium bowl, combine the BBQ sauce, soy sauce, pepper, and garlic powder. Set aside.

COOK THE CHICKEN WINGS: In a medium heavy-bottomed pot, add enough oil to come up 2 inches in the pot. Heat the oil over medium-high heat. Deep-fry the wings six to eight at a time for 8 to 10 minutes, until they are golden brown. Remove the wings from the oil and transfer to a baking sheet lined with paper towel to absorb excess oil. The wings can be kept warm in a 200°F oven while you cook the remainder.

Add as much of the sauce as you wish, and serve. We like them sticky and saucy.

Fried Chicken Wings

Angus An

❝ These are my son, Aidan's, favourite chicken wings. As a chef, watching him grow up around food has been a pleasure; seeing his palate develop, and how he learns to differentiate between flavours and really appreciate them, has been a privilege. However sophisticated he thinks his palate has gotten over the years though, he always comes back to this recipe. You make a light slurry for frying the wings, which makes them light and airy while immensely crispy—and it also makes them gluten-free! **❞**

SERVES 4
PREP TIME: 10 minutes
COOK TIME: 7 minutes

TOASTED CHILI POWDER

1 cup dried Thai bird's eye chilies

CHICKEN WINGS

16 cups canola oil

12 chicken wings

Coarse sea salt, to taste

White pepper, to taste

1 cup cornstarch

1½ cups water

½ tsp sugar

1 tbsp finely sliced pak chi farang, to garnish (see Note)

Your desired dipping sauce, to serve

MAKE THE CHILI POWDER: In a wok over medium heat, dry-toast the chilies, constantly tossing the wok to prevent them from burning. Keep tossing until the chilies turn dark red/borderline black. (At this point, you'll start to have issues holding back coughs—that's when you know they're properly toasted.) Remove from the wok, and pound with a mortar and pestle into a powder. Be extra careful not to accidentally inhale the chili powder while you're grinding it. Store in an airtight container at room temperature for up to 2 weeks.

MAKE THE CHICKEN WINGS: In a large heavy-bottomed pot over medium-high heat, preheat the oil to 350°F. Season the chicken wings with a pinch each of salt and pepper.

In a bowl, whisk the cornstarch and water together until they form a slurry resembling whole milk. Dip each wing in the slurry until evenly coated, then gently lower into the pot, one by one. Fry for 7 minutes, until the wings are golden brown and crispy. Remove from the oil and transfer to a rack lined with paper towel to absorb excess oil.

Season with the sugar, ½ tsp of the toasted chili powder, and some more salt. Garnish with pak chi farang and serve with your choice of dipping sauce.

NOTE: Pak chi farang is also known as Vietnamese coriander, or sawtooth coriander. If you can't find it, use regular coriander or green onion.

Creole Cigars

Ralph Alerte Desamours & Lee-Anne Millaire Lafleur

66 Our children love any kind of Chinese food, and this was a fun way to combine the crunch of traditional spring rolls with Caribbean flavours. Also, they have a blast frying the leftover spring roll wrappers and making chips. **99**

MAKES 24 ROLLS
PREP TIME: 30 minutes
COOK TIME: 1 hour

2 carrots, chopped

1 onion, chopped

½ bunch cilantro

2 cloves garlic

1 habanero pepper (optional)

454 g (1 lb) ground beef

1 cup imitation crab (goberge)

½ cup freshwater shrimp or small shrimp, peeled

½ cup bay scallops

3 tbsp tomato paste

1 tsp salt

1 egg

1 package spring roll wrappers

4 cups vegetable oil, for frying

In a food processor, pulse the carrots, onions, cilantro, garlic, and habanero until they are finely chopped. Transfer the vegetable mixture to a large pot.

Add the beef, imitation crab, shrimp, scallops, tomato paste, and salt. Cook over medium heat, stirring frequently, until the liquid has evaporated and the beef is fully cooked, about 30 minutes. Let cool.

In a small bowl, whisk the egg.

On a clean work surface, lay out the spring roll wrappers. Place about ½ cup of the filling mixture in the centre of the wrapper. Form the mixture into a tube, bring the ends in toward the centre, and roll into a spring roll shape, using the egg to seal the edge. Continue with the remaining wrappers.

In a deep heavy-bottomed or cast-iron pan, heat the oil to 350°F. Fry the cigars a few at a time until golden brown, about 5 minutes. The cigars can be kept warm in a 200°F oven while you cook the remainder.

Slice the cigars vertically if you like. Serve with your choice of dipping sauce and—if your kids will eat it—a salad.

Store any unfried cigars in an airtight container in the freezer for up to 3 months.

Lumpia Shanghai

Tita Flips

❝ Every time I make this recipe, my little girls jump in to help. There's something so sweet about how seriously they take this task. From helping to chop the ingredients to rolling and folding each roll, they stay so focused, and it's interesting to observe how they work. You can definitely see their individual personalities when they're engrossed in each task. And the sense of accomplishment and pride they beam with when we pull the finished hot and crispy treats out is priceless. ❞

MAKES 40 TO 50 ROLLS
PREP TIME: 1 hour
COOK TIME: 1 hour 40 minutes

454 g (1 lb) ground pork

1 medium carrot, minced

1 small onion, minced

1 clove garlic, minced

1½ tsp salt

1 tsp pepper

1 egg

½ cup dried breadcrumbs

10-inch spring roll wrappers, cut into 4 square pieces

Vegetable oil, for frying

In a large bowl, combine the pork, carrots, onions, garlic, salt, pepper, egg, and breadcrumbs. Using your hands or a sturdy wooden spoon, mix until the ingredients are homogeneous.

Place a few wrappers on a flat work surface. Place about 1 tablespoon of the filling in a line down the centre of each wrapper. Fold the bottom edge of the wrapper up toward the centre. Fold both sides of the wrapper in toward the centre. Lightly moisten the top edge of the wrapper and fold it down to seal the roll. Repeat with the remaining wrappers.

Heat the oil (deep enough to cover the rolls) in a deep skillet or pot over medium heat. Fry four to six rolls at a time until they are golden brown, turning as necessary, about 10 minutes. Transfer to a paper-towel-lined plate to drain the excess oil. The rolls can be kept warm in a 200°F oven while you cook the remainder. Serve with a sweet chili sauce, sweet and sour sauce, or plum sauce. Store in an airtight container in the fridge for up to 3 days, or in the freezer for up to 3 months.

Marinade

Marie Fitrion

“ My stepdaughter, Addison, is obsessed with dumplings (she used to call them "dunklings" when she was a toddler). Recently, I started making her Haitian-style dumplings called marinade. While they can be made with chicken, cod, or vegetarian-style, I make mine with pork belly as an homage to the canned-ham version my dad would use when I was a kid. Marinades are sometimes served alongside a Haitian street-food medley called fritay. The ones I grew up eating were flat and crispy, but my kids prefer when I make them into balls instead (they tend to be light and chewy this way, and the method forces me to work on my quenelle skills). When I am pressed for time (or oil), I stick the batter in my waffle iron. **”**

MAKES 25 TO 30 FRITTERS
PREP TIME: 20 minutes
COOK TIME: 15 minutes

¾ cup diced pork belly

1 cup all-purpose flour

½ tsp baking powder

Pinch baking soda

¼ to ½ tsp salt

¼ tsp pepper

⅔ cup water

Juice of ½ lime

1 egg, beaten

1 green onion, chopped

1 tsp chopped flat-leaf parsley

½ to 1 tsp habanero or Scotch bonnet pepper, minced (optional)

2 cups vegetable oil, for frying

In a medium skillet over medium heat, sauté the pork belly until the fat renders and the meat begins to caramelize, stirring to prevent scorching. Lower the heat, if necessary. Cook the pork thoroughly, then remove from the heat and set aside.

In a medium bowl, combine the flour, baking powder, baking soda, salt, and pepper. Set aside.

In another medium bowl, whisk together the water, lime juice, egg, green onions, parsley, and habanero or Scotch bonnet. Add this mixture to the dry ingredients and whisk to combine.

Place the pork belly in a food processor and pulse to mince. Add the minced pork with its fat to the bowl and mix well.

Heat the oil in a deep fryer or a deep skillet to 350°F. Drop the batter into the oil in 2-tablespoon-sized balls and fry until golden, turning as necessary about 5 minutes. They will expand as they fry, so do not crowd them in the fryer.

Transfer to a paper-towel-lined baking sheet to soak up any excess oil, and sprinkle them with salt. The fritters can be kept warm in a 200°F oven while you cook the remainder. If storing, let cool first and store in an airtight container between layers of waxed paper or parchment in the fridge for up to 3 days.

Vegetarian Mains

Over the past few years, I've been trying to make more vegetarian meals for my family. It hasn't always been easy, as sometimes turning to my default chicken recipe repertoire is so incredibly tempting, but for our health, our children's health, and the health of the planet, we should all be eating a more plant-based diet, period. The good news is that all of these vegetarian recipes are amazing, delicious, and most importantly, tried, tested, and kid-approved. Plus, the whole family will enjoy them—promise!

Kevin McCallister Neapolitan-Style Pizza

Janice Tiefenbach & Ryan Gray

❝ In the early '90s, pizza was pizza until Pizza Hut came to my suburban neighbourhood and introduced its deep-dish pan pizza. After that, pizza was treat food, reserved for birthdays or a really good report card. As far as I can remember, nobody ever thought about what was IN a pizza, only what was ON a pizza. At Elena, our pizza is made with naturally leavened dough made with fresh-milled organic local flour and topped with local and seasonal ingredients. As the parent of a toddler, Sloane, who is a particularly picky eater, I always feel good about serving our pizza to her because of this, sometimes even a few times a week (the perks of owning a pizza place). Usually Sloane has a Rossa, simply tomato sauce, oregano, and garlic. For special occasions, however, she gets a Kevin McCallister, our ode to the '90s-style pizzas of my youth. –Ryan **❞**

MAKES FOUR 12-INCH PIZZAS
PREP TIME: 2 hours + 48 hours resting
COOK TIME: 12 minutes per pizza

4 cups all-purpose flour

¼ cup whole wheat flour

Scant 2 cups water, at 65°F

1¼ tsp instant yeast

1 tbsp sea salt

Olive oil

2 cups tomato sauce of your choice (we like Bianco DiNapoli)

4 cups shredded mozzarella

In the bowl of a stand mixer or in a large bowl, combine the flours and water and mix on low speed for 4 minutes, or by hand for 8 minutes. Let rest for 20 minutes. Add the yeast and salt and continue mixing for 9 to 12 minutes, until the dough is supple and homogeneous.

Transfer to an oiled container. With your hand under the dough at the farthest edge, fold the dough over and onto itself. Rotate the container 90 degrees and fold the dough again, repeating this twice more for a total of four folds. Cover the dough and let rest 30 minutes. Repeat two times, allowing 30 minutes between each set of folds, for a total of 1½ hours resting. This is referred to as the "bulk ferment."

Transfer the dough to a lightly floured work surface and divide into four even pieces. Shape into smooth balls, being careful not to tear the dough. Place the balls in a lightly oiled and floured container. Store, covered, in the fridge for 2 days to allow the dough to ferment and develop more flavour and complexity (over time the texture of the dough will change, as it relaxes and proofs a bit, which gives it a very different character when it bakes, in look, taste, and texture). If not making pizzas right away, the dough can be stored for another day in an airtight container in the fridge.

Allow the dough to come to room temperature for 20 minutes before stretching.

Place a baking stone in the oven (see Note on page 98). Preheat the oven to 500°F.

Continued

Carefully cut the edges of the dough balls to separate them and transfer to a well-floured surface. Handle the dough carefully; you don't want to cause any holes as you move it, and you want to try to preserve as round a shape as possible. It is also important to keep the top and bottom always in the same orientation. Make sure both the top and bottom are well floured before beginning to stretch out.

Stretch your dough out flat on a clean countertop. Try to keep air in what will become the crust. Avoid compressing the dough around the edges as much as possible. Begin by pressing a rough round shape inside the dough, respecting about a 1½-inch border, which will become your crust. Once you have established the inner ring, gently press down the dough inside the ring. Gradually begin stretching the dough out in a circular motion. Add more flour underneath the dough as necessary to reach a diameter of 12 inches. Transfer the dough to a piece of parchment paper.

The Kevin McCallister is a very simple pizza: only sauce and cheese! Spread ½ cup of the tomato sauce per pizza evenly toward the crust in a clockwise motion, then sprinkle 1 cup of the cheese on top evenly.

Slide the pizza and parchment paper directly onto the baking stone and bake for 8 to 12 minutes until ready. You can also broil the top for the last few minutes to mimic the doming effect of a wood oven. Repeat for your remaining pizzas.

NOTE: A warmer dough is faster to stretch out but is more susceptible to holes. A cold dough is less susceptible to tearing, but takes more effort to work out because the dough is less relaxed.

If you don't have a baking stone, you can use a baking sheet for the first 8 minutes of baking the pizza, then transfer the pizza directly to the grill rack once the dough is set for the final few minutes.

Barlow's Egg Noodle & Broccoli Carbonara

Cory Vitiello

f This dish works 100% of the time with my son, Barlow. I try to vary his meals as much as possible; however, when it's been a long day and we need a sure thing that is easy and satiating for him, believe me, we are making this. This is a bastardized hack job of a carbonara recipe and by no means traditional—feel free to make any additions or modifications that may suit your own kid's eating habits. ™

SERVES 4
PREP TIME: 5 minutes
COOK TIME: 10 minutes

200 g (7 oz) dried egg noodles (our go-to is tagliatelle, but use your kid's favourite shape)

4 cups chopped broccoli florets

½ cup grated Parmesan, plus more to serve, if desired

4 eggs

2 tbsp olive oil

2 tbsp heavy cream

Salt and pepper, to taste

Bring a small pot of salted water to a boil. Add the pasta and broccoli and cook the pasta according to package directions (see Note).

Meanwhile, in a bowl, combine the Parmesan, eggs, olive oil, and cream.

When ready, strain the pasta, reserving a tablespoon or so of the cooking water to finish the sauce. Working off the heat, transfer the pasta and broccoli back to the pot, add the cheese mixture and some reserved cooking water, and stir quickly to form a creamy sauce. Season to taste with salt and pepper. Allow to cool slightly.

Serve, finished with a bit of extra grated cheese, if desired. Let your kid go to town slurping away. They will love it!

NOTE: We use noodles that cook rather quickly (6 to 7 minutes), and we cook it at the same time as the broccoli because who needs extra dishes when you're cooking for your kid?

Spaghetti with Garlic Rapini

Rebecca Wolfe

66 This is a family favourite of ours that my kids absolutely love and never get sick of. It's so simple to make, it's fast, and it's a great way to get them to eat some greens. 99

SERVES 4
PREP TIME: 10 minutes
COOK TIME: 20 minutes

1 to 2 bunches rapini or your favourite greens, cleaned and roughly chopped

2 tsp salt

225 g (½ lb) whole wheat spaghetti or other favourite pasta

2 tbsp olive oil

5 cloves garlic, thinly sliced or crushed

2 tbsp grated Parmesan

1 tbsp pine nuts, toasted

In a large pot of boiling water, blanch the rapini until tender, about 3 minutes. Remove from the water and set aside. In the same boiling water, add the salt and pasta. Cook the pasta according to the package directions. Drain, reserving a bit of cooking liquid.

Meanwhile, in a large heavy-bottomed skillet (like cast iron) over medium heat, heat the oil. Add the garlic and cook for 30 seconds. Add the rapini and cook with the garlic for about 4 to 5 minutes, stirring frequently. Add the pasta and toss with the rapini.

If the pasta begins to stick, add a bit of the reserved cooking liquid and mix to loosen the pasta (or add a bit of white wine). Season to taste.

Transfer the pasta to a serving platter and top with the Parmesan and pine nuts. Serve immediately!

Vegan Mac & Cheese

Adrian Forte

66 "Boring," "weird," and "yucky." These are just a few of the terms I've overheard children using to describe food. My girlfriend's 10-year-old sister, Kaitlin, had a long list of reasons why she didn't like certain ingredients. She couldn't tolerate any herbs or spices and she didn't consume any animal proteins, but she also disliked most leafy vegetables and hated the texture of beans and legumes. This didn't leave me with much room for creativity. I made it my personal responsibility to get her to eat something other than plain oatmeal, white rice, and tofu. Then I discovered that a really good sauce is the key to getting kids to eat anything! Cashew cream tzatziki, miso and maple glaze, coconut cream alfredo, raspberry vinaigrette—these are just a few of the plant-based sauces I developed to satisfy Kaitlin's taste buds while including some nutrient-dense ingredients that many kids dislike. 99

SERVES 4

PREP TIME: 10 minutes
 + a few hours soaking
COOK TIME: 35 minutes

½ cup cashews

225 g (½ lb) sweet potatoes, peeled and cubed

½ cup coconut milk, plus more if needed

3 cloves garlic, peeled

¼ cup nutritional yeast

Salt and pepper, to taste

2 cups elbow macaroni

Soak the cashews in water for a few hours, then strain.

In a medium pot of boiling water, cook the sweet potatoes until tender, about 10 minutes. Drain and reserve.

In another medium pot, combine the cashews and coconut milk and bring to a simmer. Simmer over low heat for 5 to 8 minutes until soft. Let cool for 5 minutes; do not drain.

Place the cooked sweet potatoes in a food processor and add the cashews and coconut milk. Pulse until smooth. Add the garlic and nutritional yeast and pulse until emulsified. Season to taste with salt and pepper, adding extra coconut milk, if needed, to adjust the consistency.

In a large pot of boiling salted water, cook the macaroni until al dente. Drain the macaroni and add it to the sauce, stirring to combine. Serve immediately.

Classic Mac & Cheese

Joe Friday

❝ Cooking for kids is one of my favourite pastimes, and two of my favourite little ones are my friends' children, sisters Julia and Rachael. They are so curious and love all sorts of food. Usually I make them a pretty elevated mac and cheese to cater to their great pallets. This is a special recipe that I got from my mom, Debra Friday (over the years I've added different types of cheese for variation, but it has the same heart behind it), and it's excellent for dinner parties with kids because, you know children, they love cheese! I present to you the only mac and cheese you will ever need. Enjoy! ❞

SERVES 6
PREP TIME: 30 minutes
COOK TIME: 1 hour

454 g (1 lb) elbow macaroni
  or your preferred pasta

Olive oil

½ cup butter

½ cup all-purpose flour

4 cups milk

½ cup chicken or vegetable stock
  (optional)

1 tbsp onion powder

1 tsp chili powder

½ cup sour cream

½ cup cream cheese

2 egg yolks

3 cups shredded 2-year-old
  cheddar

1 cup shredded Gruyère

1 cup shredded Monterey Jack

1 cup grated Pecorino Romano

Salt, to taste

Preheat the oven to 325°F. Butter a 9 × 13-inch baking dish. Set aside.

Bring a large pot of salted water to a boil. Add the pasta and cook for 1 minute less than the package directions for al dente. Drain the pasta and toss with a bit of olive oil to prevent sticking.

In a large saucepan over medium heat, melt the butter. Add the flour and whisk to combine. The mixture will look like wet sand. Cook for 1 minute, whisking constantly. Slowly add half of the milk, whisking constantly until smooth. Slowly add the remaining milk, whisking constantly again until smooth. Cook over medium heat, whisking often, until the sauce has thickened. It should be the consistency of a thinned-out condensed soup; if you've thickened it too much, add some stock to thin it out. Add the spices and stir to combine.

In a large bowl, combine the sour cream, cream cheese, and egg yolks and whisk to combine. In a separate bowl, combine the four cheeses. Add half of these shredded cheese to the sour cream mixture, and set the rest aside.

Add half of the sour cream mixture to the saucepan and stir until completely melted into the sauce. Add the remaining sour cream mixture and stir until smooth. Season to taste with salt. Add the pasta and mix until completely covered in the sauce.

Transfer half of the pasta and sauce to the prepared baking dish and top with half of the remaining shredded cheese. Add the rest of the pasta and sauce and top with the remaining shredded cheese.

Bake for 30 minutes, or until the top is oozing and melted. Let rest for 10 minutes before serving.

Leafy Green Pesto

Emma Cardarelli

66 I found it difficult to incorporate healthy greens into my daughter Rose's diet until I discovered her love of pesto! It was also a seamless way to start to include nuts in her diet. This is easily her favourite meal. Using basil and greens grown in my back garden in the summer, it's a quick and delicious meal that I know she will eat and enjoy. It can be messy, but it's worth it! **99**

SERVES 4
PREP TIME: 10 minutes
COOK TIME: 10 minutes

1 cup tightly packed fresh
    basil leaves

1 cup tightly packed kale, spinach,
    or any other leafy green

¾ cup olive oil

½ cup pine nuts, lightly toasted,
    or toasted pumpkin seeds

⅓ cup grated Parmesan, plus
    more to serve

2 cloves roasted garlic (optional)

2 cups whole wheat pasta

3 tbsp frozen peas

Photo also shows
Chickpea Patties, page 122

In a food processor, blend the basil, greens, olive oil, pine nuts, Parmesan, and garlic until homogeneous. You can make this as smooth or chunky as you like. I usually blend it until the pine nuts are ground to the size of a grain of sand. It is always helpful to stop halfway through blending to scrape the sides of the bowl with a rubber spatula to make the mixture uniform.

Bring a medium pot of salted water to a boil. Add the pasta and cook according to the package directions. Strain, reserving about ¼ cup of the cooking water. Return the reserved cooking water to the pot, add the peas, and cook for 2 to 3 minutes. Add the cooked pasta and half of the pesto. Mix thoroughly. Serve.

Place the remaining pesto in a small zip-lock bag, press it flat, and freeze it for up to 1 month. When packed this way, it thaws quickly when you need to use it.

Gnocchi di Ricotta

Rob Gentile

66 My daughter, Clarice, came into the world with a very particular palate. Like most 4-year-olds, she's super picky and strictly adheres to what I like to call a "beige" diet. Her number-one request is "Pasta with no sauce, Papa?" because she doesn't like anything too colourful, so this recipe is perfect for her and she loves it. On top of that, the gnocchi are finished with butter and cheese, so not only do they taste great, they're also up to Clarice's standards and the ingredients are packed with protein for growing kids who are particular about what they eat.

This dish is also my way of getting her involved because, like her dad, she gets super excited about anything having to do with pasta and making it by hand. Making gnocchi is the ideal intro for anyone who wants to make pasta from scratch because it's easy and fun and there's little chance for error. The beauty about gnocchi is that you don't have to be super methodical; they can be different shapes and the dough isn't delicate, so it can be handled in every which way and still be perfect. Most kids who grew up in an Italian household (including myself) spent a lot of their childhood rolling and cutting gnocchi—it's like the playdough of pasta. 99

SERVES 4
PREP TIME: 20 minutes
COOK TIME: 2 to 3 minutes

1 cup ricotta, drained in a sieve
    to remove excess water

½ cup grated Pecorino Romano

1 egg yolk

1 tsp salt

¾ cup all-purpose flour

Butter, to serve

Grated Parmesan, to serve

In a medium bowl, combine the ricotta, Pecorino, egg yolk, and salt and whisk to combine. Add the flour and mix until just combined.

Transfer the dough to a lightly floured work surface and divide the dough in half. Roll into long tubes about ½ inch thick. Cut into ½-inch-long pieces and roll over a gnocchi board to add ridges (optional). As you shape the pieces, transfer them to a lightly floured baking sheet.

Bring a large pot of salted water to a boil. Add the gnocchi and stir once to prevent sticking. Boil until they begin to float, about 2 to 3 minutes. Drain and serve immediately tossed in butter and topped with grated Parmesan.

Pesto Pappardelle

Chuck Hughes

66 This is a fun thing I like to do with my two boys on a Saturday. We make the pasta in the morning, and then we all eat it together at night. Not only do they learn how to make this dish, pasta and all, but they see how simple it is too. Plus, it always gets a little messy—which they love—and we have a really good time. The best part? They truly love this dish so they're always asking to make it. 99

SERVES 4 TO 6

PREP TIME: 30 minutes + 30 minutes to overnight resting

COOK TIME: 5 minutes

PASTA

2 cups all-purpose flour

1 tsp fine sea salt

4 eggs

1 egg yolk

3 tbsp olive oil

PESTO

5 cups fresh basil leaves

1 cup celery leaves

3 cloves garlic

1 cup grated Grana Padano, plus more to serve

2 cups olive oil

½ tsp sea salt

Pepper, to taste

Lemon zest, to taste

Grated Grana Padano, to serve

Photo on page 112

MAKE THE PASTA: In a medium bowl, combine the flour and salt. Transfer to a clean work surface and make a well in the centre of the flour. Add the eggs, egg yolk, and oil to the centre and mix with a fork until it begins to come together. Knead for 5 minutes. Wrap in plastic wrap and let rest for 30 minutes, or up to overnight, in the fridge.

Let the dough come to room temperature for 20 minutes before rolling. Place the dough on a lightly floured work surface. Using a pasta maker, roll the pasta dough until it is almost paper thin. You might need to do this in batches. Roll up the pasta sheets and trim them so they are even. Cut into 1-inch-wide noodles.

Bring a large pot of salted water to a boil. Cook the pasta until tender, about 3 to 4 minutes. Drain, reserving ½ cup pasta water.

MAKE THE PESTO: Place all the ingredients in a food processor and blend until very smooth.

Place the pesto in a large saucepan over medium heat. Add the pasta and toss to coat, adding the reserved pasta water 1 tablespoon at a time to thin the sauce. Serve with freshly grated Grana Padano.

NOTE: You can use dried pasta for this recipe, but I like making it fresh with my boys.

Green Hulk Risotto

Dyan Solomon

❝ I don't have kids myself, but I definitely love Sarahmée, my business partner Eric's daughter. Eric and his family are basically family to me, so when I get a chance to cook for these lovelies, I make things we can all eat: "adult" food, but not too weird to freak out the little one (lucky for me, so far Sarahmée eats absolutely everything). This recipe has a nice dose of greens and is very vibrant in colour. That's the real draw for kids: it's not a "vegetable" green, but more of a "Hulk" green—a huge difference in a child's mindset, so be sure to mention this a couple of times. And once they put it in their mouths (fingers crossed), they'll realize this risotto is creamy, cheesy, and very comforting. Just tell them it will make them grow up big and strong, like the Hulk! And if that doesn't work, bribe them with my cookies for dessert (page 209). ❞

SERVES 4 TO 6
PREP TIME: 30 minutes
COOK TIME: 30 minutes

RISOTTO

¼ cup butter, plus more to serve

1 small shallot, finely chopped

2 cloves garlic, minced

1 cup arborio rice

¼ cup white wine

2 cups hot vegetable or chicken stock, plus more to serve

1½ tsp salt

Pepper

PURÉE

1 container baby spinach (about 150 g/5 oz)

1 bunch flat-leaf parsley

Zest of 4 lemons

3 cloves garlic, finely grated

½ tsp pepper

½ cup olive oil

Grated Parmesan, to taste

Lemon juice, to taste

MAKE THE RISOTTO: In a medium pot over medium heat, melt the butter. Add the shallots and garlic and cook until translucent. Add the rice and cook, stirring, until the grains are coated and translucent. Add the wine and reduce until the rice is almost dry.

Add a ladleful of stock and continue cooking, stirring all the while, until the liquid has been absorbed. Continue adding the remaining stock, waiting until the liquid has been absorbed before adding more. When the rice is just slightly undercooked, season with salt and pepper and transfer to a baking sheet. Place in the fridge to stop the cooking.

MAKE THE PURÉE: In a pot of boiling salted water, blanch the spinach and parsley. Wring them dry in a clean dish towel to remove the excess water. Roughly chop the greens and place them in the bowl of a food processor. Add the lemon zest, garlic, pepper, and oil. Process until the greens are puréed. Place the mixture in a metal bowl set over an ice bath to keep the colour vibrant. Pass through a sieve if the purée is stringy.

TO SERVE: In a medium pot, gently heat the cold rice with a pat of butter and a ladleful of stock. Add the green purée, grated Parmesan, and lemon juice to taste. Taste and adjust the seasoning as needed and serve.

Lentil Risotto

Michele Forgione

❝ My eldest son, Giovanni, has never been into "junky" food, despite the fact that I own a casse-croûte (snack bar) with all the fries, hot dogs, and hamburgers any kid could ever want! He really cares about what he eats and loves home-cooked meals. When he was younger, I would always make him one of his favourites on my day off: lentil soup. He adored it, and I could never make enough. Then, one day while I was preparing him a big batch, I messed up the ratio of rice to stock, adding way too much rice. It literally sucked up all the soup's liquid and became a big pot of mush (chefs make mistakes too!). I had no choice but to break it to my son. "Giovanni, I'm so sorry, Daddy put way too much rice in your soup and now it looks like a risotto." As I braced myself for disappointment, he looked at it, took a bite, and started gobbling it up like crazy. Since then, I've turned his favourite lentil soup into a proper risotto, and to this day it's still the dish he always asks me to make. **❞**

SERVES 4 TO 6
PREP TIME: 10 minutes
COOK TIME: 35 minutes

⅓ cup small dry green lentils, rinsed

2 tbsp olive oil

3 tbsp butter, diced

1 onion, finely chopped

½ cup diced mild pancetta

2 cloves garlic, finely chopped

Salt and pepper, to taste

1¼ cups carnaroli rice

½ cup dry white wine

3⅓ cups warm chicken stock

¼ cup finely grated Parmesan, plus more to serve

In a small saucepan, combine the lentils and enough cold water to cover them generously, and bring to a boil. Cook until the lentils are half-cooked, about 6 to 8 minutes. Drain and set aside.

Meanwhile, in a large saucepan over medium heat, heat the oil and half the butter. Add the onions, pancetta, and garlic, season to taste, and sauté until the onions are tender and the pancetta is crisp, 5 to 6 minutes.

Add the rice, stir to coat, and lightly toast for 1 to 2 minutes. Add the wine and stir until reduced by half, then add the lentils and stir to combine.

Add the warm stock, a ladleful at a time, stirring constantly until all the liquid is absorbed before adding more. Continue stirring and adding stock until the rice is al dente and the lentils are tender, about 15 to 20 minutes.

When it's ready, remove the risotto from the heat and add the Parmesan and the remaining butter. Season to taste and serve immediately with love and extra Parmesan, if desired.

Turmeric Rice with Mango & Edamame

Meeru Dhalwala

❝ I used to call this the "tricky rice" because we used a simple turmeric rice to "trick" our girls into trying other foods on top. My husband, Vikram Vij, and I involved our girls in cooking as much as possible while they were growing up. We started them on this recipe at as young as 3 years old—providing backup help with draining rice and using a knife. Then we let them choose what they wanted as toppings and add as much as they wanted to their rice. This dish is very adaptable; the turmeric gives it a fun yellow colour that matches so many foods. We've tried countless combinations, but now, as adults, my daughters remember this mango and edamame combination the most. If you don't have mango, you can use peaches or nectarines, or switch from fruit to savoury foods such as tofu, thawed peas, or chickpeas if you'd like. Let your child use their imagination to add their own favourite foods. We always use lemon and cilantro as the final topping for a beautiful combination of yellows and greens (for the grown-ups, we also recommend some jalapeño or crushed cayenne pepper). **❞**

SERVES 6

PREP TIME: 15 minutes plus 1 hour soaking

COOK TIME: 15 minutes

1½ cups basmati rice, rinsed and drained twice with cold water

2⅔ cups water

2 tbsp ghee

1½ tsp ground turmeric

1 tsp salt

1 bunch green onions, finely chopped

Juice of ½ lemon (optional)

⅔ cup finely chopped cilantro, stems included + more for garnish (optional)

1 to 2 mangoes, peeled, pitted, and chopped

2 cups frozen edamame, cooked according to package instructions and drained

In a medium bowl, combine the rice with the water and let soak for 1 hour. What makes basmati precious is how it lengthens, and it only lengthens if you soak it.

In a heavy-bottomed pot over medium-high heat, melt the ghee and immediately add the turmeric and salt. Stir and add the green onions. Sauté for 1 minute, then remove from the heat.

In a small bowl, combine the lemon juice and chopped cilantro. Transfer to a serving bowl.

Once the rice has finished soaking, pour it and the soaking water into the pot with the green onions. Bring to a boil over high heat, reduce the heat to a simmer, cover, and cook for 10 minutes. Remove the pot from the heat and let the rice sit for 3 to 5 minutes.

To serve, spoon the rice into serving bowls. Place small dishes filled with the other toppings around the table so the kids can garnish their own dish.

NOTE: We use basmati rice from either Pakistan or India, the real deal, but you can also use whatever staple rice your family enjoys. As per Ayurvedic scripture, this dish tastes great with ghee (clarified butter). The process of making ghee is to boil unsalted butter gently and remove the milk solids with a strainer as they separate (making ghee lactose-free). We follow no specific diet but are a mostly vegetarian family who love to accent the milder Indian foods with ghee. You can buy ghee, but I recommend that you make it at home following one of the many simple recipes online.

Green Onion Oil Noodles

Anita Feng

❝ I left China and my grandparents at the age of 10 to join my parents and my little sister who had already settled down in Montreal. I kept my habit of having noodles for breakfast, which was a bit more time-consuming to make, but my dad would always take care of it. I'm a sleepyhead and a slow person in the morning; my dad would prepare my noodles ready to go with my chopsticks so I could eat them in the car while he drove me to school. Green onion oil noodles are my all-time favourite, and even now I make them for staff meals in any restaurant that I work in. **❞**

SERVES 4
PREP TIME: 5 minutes
COOK TIME: 10 minutes

1¼ cups vegetable oil

2 bunches green onions, cut
    into 4, green and white parts
    separated

½ cup sliced fresh ginger

2 shallots, sliced

10 cloves garlic, smashed

¾ cup light soy sauce

¼ cup dark soy sauce

6 tbsp sugar

400 g (14 oz) dried noodles
    of your choice

4 fried eggs (optional)

**Photo also shows Braised Pork
& Shiitake Meatballs, page 173**

In a small pot over medium heat, heat the oil. Check the temperature with a wooden chopstick; when small bubbles appear around the chopstick, the oil is ready. Add the white parts of the green onions, ginger, shallots, and garlic. Reduce the heat to low and stir-fry until golden. Remove the solid pieces and discard them.

Add the green parts of the green onions to the oil and stir-fry until golden and fragrant, being careful not to burn them. Take the pot off the heat. Remove the green onions and set aside.

Add the soy sauces and sugar to the pot and stir to dissolve the sugar. Add the green onions back in and stir to combine. This oil is best if made ahead of time to give the flavours time to concentrate, and keeps well in the fridge for up to 1 week.

Bring a medium pot of water to a boil and cook the noodles according to the package instructions. Drain the noodles and transfer them to a serving bowl. Add a few spoonfuls of the green onion oil along with some pieces of the fried green onions. Mix well and serve. You can top each serving of noodles with a fried egg, if desired.

Chickpea Patties

Emma Cardarelli

❝ These chickpea patties are an amalgamation of a couple of different recipes. I wanted to introduce my daughter, Rose, to legumes early in her life, as they are so high in nutritional value. I never ate them when I was young, so it took me a long time to come around to them later in life. These patties are packed with all kinds of healthy ingredients that I think are important for kids to be introduced to at a young age. **❞**

SERVES 4 TO 6
PREP TIME: 20 minutes
COOK TIME: 15 minutes

3 tbsp olive oil

3 medium café mushrooms, diced

1 small onion, diced

2 cloves garlic, minced

1 (540 ml/19 oz) can chickpeas, drained and rinsed

1 McIntosh apple, grated

⅓ cup grated Parmesan

2 tbsp flaxseeds, ground

½ tsp ground cumin

Salt and pepper, to taste

½ cup almond powder (ground almonds)

Photo on page 109

In a medium skillet over medium heat, heat 2 tablespoons of the oil. Add the mushrooms and sauté until brown, then add the onions and cook until translucent, about 5 minutes. Add the garlic and cook for 2 minutes. Remove from the heat and let cool.

Place the chickpeas in the bowl of a food processor. Pulse until they are coarsely chopped but not puréed. Transfer the chickpeas to a large bowl and add the cooled vegetables, and the apple, Parmesan, flax, and cumin. Mix well and season to taste with salt and pepper. Add the almond powder and stir to combine.

If you're planning to freeze the patties to cook later: Using a small ice-cream scoop or a tablespoon, scoop the mixture onto a parchment-paper-lined baking sheet, then press them into patties. Freeze on the baking sheet until solid, then transfer to a sealable bag in the freezer for up to 1 month. Thaw before cooking.

Otherwise, use the same method to scoop the mixture and press it into patties on the countertop. To cook, heat the remaining oil in a skillet over medium heat and cook the patties, working in batches as necessary, until brown on both sides, about 5 minutes.

NOTE: You can also use ground chicken thighs or ground pork instead of chickpeas. If you do, omit the almond powder and cumin and instead use ground sage and ginger to make them taste like breakfast sausages.

Cauliflower Cheese Bake

Suzanne Barr

❝ This is my go-to for the whole family when I don't have a lot of time but still want to serve something substantial, and itis the epitome of comfort food. As a chef and mother, I try to tweak hearty classics to make them healthier without losing any of the yum factor. My son Myles has no idea that this cheesy fave has cauliflower in it, and I'm okay with that. I like using panko breadcrumbs to sprinkle on top—he loves that crunchy component before digging into the cheesy, gooey goodness. ❞

SERVES 4
PREP TIME: 20 minutes
COOK TIME: 50 minutes

1½ heads cauliflower

2 tbsp olive oil

½ cup medium-diced white onion

½ cup medium-diced carrot

¼ tsp salt, plus more to taste

3 cups vegetable stock

3 cups shredded sharp cheddar

½ cup coconut milk

½ tsp apple cider vinegar

½ tsp Dijon mustard

¼ tsp ground nutmeg

¼ tsp cayenne pepper

2 cups panko breadcrumbs

¼ cup chopped flat-leaf parsley

1 tsp pepper, plus more to taste

Photo on page 125

Roughly chop the ½ head cauliflower and set aside.

In a large pot over medium heat, heat the olive oil. Add the onions, carrots, and salt and cook, stirring occasionally, until the onions are soft and translucent, about 5 to 7 minutes.

Add the chopped cauliflower and stock and increase the heat to high. Cover the pot and let cook, stirring occasionally, until the cauliflower is soft, about 10 to 15 minutes. Remove from the heat.

Meanwhile, cut the remaining whole cauliflower into ¼-inch-thick slices and place the slices in a casserole dish.

Preheat the oven to 375°F.

Carefully blend the cauliflower soup in the pot using a blender. It will be hot, so use caution. Once it is smooth, return it to the pot and place over medium heat. Once it begins to simmer, add 2 cups of the cheddar and whisk until smooth and creamy. Remove the pot from the heat and add the coconut milk, vinegar, mustard, nutmeg, and cayenne. Whisk to combine. Taste and adjust the seasoning as needed.

Pour enough sauce over the prepared cauliflower slices to thoroughly cover them. You might not need all the sauce. Any excess can be served as a soup or frozen for up to 3 months.

In a medium bowl, combine the panko, remaining 1 cup of cheddar, the parsley, and pepper and toss until well mixed. Sprinkle over the cauliflower and bake until the sauce is bubbly and the top is crispy and golden brown, about 30 minutes. Remove from the oven and let rest for 5 minutes before serving.

Cheese Soufflé

Jennifer Dewasha

66 My nephews, Jackson and Michael, love eggs and cheese. They are amazed with the science of food and enjoy learning new techniques in the kitchen. People tend to shy away from soufflés, thinking they are difficult, but this is far from the truth! The key is to prepare all of your ingredients before you begin the roux process, and then your kids can make the mix with your supervision. The excitement comes from anticipating the soufflé's rise in the oven and seeing your masterpiece when it comes out! Eggs that are so light, fluffy, and airy! Substitute the cheddar with any other cheeses your kids enjoy. 99

SERVES 4
PREP TIME: 10 minutes
COOK TIME: 35 minutes

4 tbsp butter

2 tbsp dried breadcrumbs

2 tbsp all-purpose flour

¾ cup milk

½ tsp salt

1 cup shredded cheddar

3 eggs, separated

1 egg white

Place a rack on the bottom third of the oven. Preheat the oven to 375°F.

Using a pastry brush, butter the bottom and sides of a 1-quart soufflé dish with 2 tablespoons of the butter. Coat the bottom and sides with the breadcrumbs, making sure the dish is evenly coated. Place in the fridge until ready to bake.

In a small saucepan over medium heat, melt the remaining 2 tablespoons of butter. Whisk in the flour and cook, stirring, until the flour is cooked but not browned, about 4 minutes. Add the milk in a steady stream, whisking all the while.

Add the salt and cook, stirring constantly, until the mixture thickens, about 4 to 5 minutes. Remove the pan from the heat and add the cheese. Whisk until the cheese is melted and the sauce is smooth. Add the egg yolks one at a time, whisking all the while before each addition.

In the bowl of a stand mixer or a medium bowl, whisk the egg whites until soft peaks form. Using a spatula, gently fold a third of the whites into the cheese mixture. Add the remaining egg whites and fold until just combined. Do not overmix. Spoon the batter into the cold soufflé dish and bake until the top is puffed and golden, about 25 minutes. Serve immediately.

Arepas

Sarah Forrester

❝ My kids have done a lot of travelling and eaten a wide variety of food over the years. When I asked them what their favourites were, they hemmed and hawed quite a bit. Ramen... lentil soup... hummus... but arepas finally won as the top pick. Arepas are popular in Columbia, Venezuela, Bolivia, and Puerto Rico. They are patties made of cornmeal, baked or fried, then stuffed with your choice of ingredients. ❞

SERVES 4
PREP TIME: 10 minutes
COOK TIME: less than 15 minutes

2 cups masa harina

1 tsp sea salt

1 tsp sesame seeds

2 cups water

2 tsp olive oil

FILLING SUGGESTIONS

Cooked black beans

Sliced avocado

Salsa

Scrambled eggs

Chopped cilantro, to garnish

In a medium bowl, combine the masa, salt, sesame seeds, and water. Mix until a dough forms. Divide into four even pieces and shape into patties ½-inch thick.

In a pot of simmering water, poach the patties until they float, about 4 minutes. Remove from the water and let dry on paper towels.

In a skillet over medium-high heat, heat the oil. Fry the patties until they are golden, about 7 minutes, turning once. When ready to serve, slice each arepa about three-quarters of the way through and stuff with your favourite fillings. Enjoy!

Zucchini Bake

Andrea Callan

66 As kids, my siblings and I were always picky about eating vegetables. My mom discovered that we all liked Italian dressing and that if she snuck some on our vegetables, we were more inclined to try them. Our gardens were always plentiful with all the produce in this recipe, which helped subsidize the food bills for a family of five. She would make this for us at least once or twice a week with a side of rice or pasta or mashed potatoes. This is an everyday recipe you can serve the same way, or as a side to chicken, white fish, pork, or steak. I get more compliments on this simple dish than almost anything else I make. If you're in a hurry, don't feel guilty about throwing it in the microwave to save time or in a pressure cooker for 5 minutes. 99

SERVES 4
PREP TIME: 10 minutes
COOK TIME: 40 minutes

1 medium zucchini, seeded and cut into ¼-inch slices on the diagonal

1 medium red bell pepper, seeded and cut into ¼-inch slices on the diagonal

2 medium tomatoes, cut into wedges, or 1 pint cherry tomatoes

½ red or white onion, cut into wedges

4 cloves garlic, thinly sliced

1 handful fresh basil or flat-leaf parsley leaves

1 tsp pepper

¼ tsp salt

½ cup Italian salad dressing

Preheat the oven to 350°F.

In a heatproof baking dish, combine all the ingredients. Cover with aluminum foil or a lid and bake for 40 minutes. You can also microwave on high for 7 to 10 minutes.

Fish & Meat Mains

I had a real moment not too long ago when my son took a huge bite of salmon, looked up at me, and said, "This is good." Fish is definitely a harder sell for my son in general, but meat-based dishes are usually a sure bet. The problem is more that we fall into a rotation routine and forget to take chances, try new recipes, and see how they go over. Am I scared of my kid throwing a fit at the dinner table and not wanting to eat? Definitely. But do you know how I got him to eat that salmon? I paired it with something that I know he likes. For that particular meal, it was mac and cheese. So, if you want your little one to try a new main meal, try serving it with a side you know they like. It might not work every time, but it's worth a try.

Accras

Ralph Alerte Desamours & Lee-Anne Millaire Lafleur

❝ These salted cod fritters were the first item our boys tasted from our restaurant Palme's menu. We often had supper with the kids there before service on days they weren't in daycare. We got to spend a little more time with them, and accras became a staple of any family meal at the restaurant. ❞

SERVES 4 TO 6
PREP TIME: 15 minutes
COOK TIME: 1 hour 15 minutes

16 cups water

500 g/1.1 lb salted cod

2 carrots

½ bunch cilantro

2 cloves garlic

1 tbsp garlic powder

1 tbsp paprika

1 tbsp ground coriander

1 tsp salt

Scotch bonnet or habanero pepper, finely chopped (optional, to bring some heat)

4 cups all-purpose flour

4 tbsp baking powder

Zest and juice of 4 limes

12 cups vegetable oil

Your favourite dipping sauce, to serve

In a large pot over medium-high heat, bring the water to a soft boil. Add the salted cod and simmer for 45 minutes. Drain, let the salted cod cool, and then shred.

In a food processor, combine the carrots, cilantro, garlic, garlic powder, paprika, coriander, and salt and purée into a paste. (The hot pepper can be added to the mixture now if the kids have a tolerance for spice.)

Transfer to a large bowl, and add the shredded salted cod, flour, baking powder, and lime zest and juice. Mix to combine until it reaches the consistency of cake batter.

In a heavy-bottomed pan or Dutch oven, heat the oil to 350°F. Using an ice-cream scoop or a large spoon, carefully scoop up the batter into balls. Working in batches, add the balls to the hot oil, being careful not to overcrowd the pan. Cook for 4 minutes, then remove using a slotted spoon, and let cool on a wire rack or paper-towel-lined plate to absorb excess oil. Repeat with the remaining batter. The accras can be kept warm in a 200°F oven while you cook the remainder.

Serve with your favourite dipping sauce, or store in an airtight container in the fridge for up to 3 days.

Lobster Pasta

Luc Doucet

66 We are so fortunate out east to have an abundance of beautiful seafood and all sorts of amazing produce. Of course, we are known for lobster, and even though we have access to it more often than most, we appreciate how lucky that is, and always love to create fun dishes with it. My son, Alexis, and I love making pasta, and this is one of his favourite meals from my restaurant Black Rabbit. So I thought, why not make it at home and spend some time doing it together? Professionally, I usually love pushing my creativity, but I also find that simple, well-made meals like this go a long way—both at the restaurant and at home. 99

SERVES 4

PREP TIME: 40 minutes + 30 minutes chilling

COOK TIME: 1 hour to 1 hour 25 minutes

DOUGH

2½ cups all-purpose flour

4 eggs, at room temperature

Pinch salt

LOBSTER & SAUCE

2 live or cooked lobsters
(about 680 g/1.1 lb each)

4 cups heavy cream

1 medium onion, chopped

1 medium carrot, finely chopped

4 dry bay leaves

2 sprigs thyme

1 tsp salt

1 tsp pepper

1 cup grated Parmesan

4 green onions, finely chopped,
to serve

MAKE THE DOUGH: On a clean work surface, heap the flour in a mound and make a depression in the centre, like a volcano. Crack the eggs into the centre of the volcano, along with the salt. Using a fork, blend the mixture slowly together, incorporating the flour a little at a time by widening the centre. Once mixed, knead the dough until smooth, about 5 minutes. Wrap in plastic wrap and refrigerate for 30 minutes to relax the dough.

COOK THE LOBSTERS AND MAKE THE SAUCE: If using live lobsters, drop the lobsters into a large pot of boiling salted water, and cook for 8 to 9 minutes. Remove the lobsters from the pot and place in a bowl of cold water to stop the cooking.

Or start here if your lobsters are cooked: Remove the meat from the tail, claws, and knuckles, setting the meat aside and reserving the shells. If you want to add extra flavour and funk (depending on the tastes of your household), add the innards to the sauce later on.

Meanwhile, in a medium pot, heat the cream over medium-low heat. Add the lobster shells (tail, claw, and knuckles only), onions, carrots, bay leaves, thyme, salt, and pepper and let simmer over low heat for 45 to 60 minutes. Strain the sauce through a fine-mesh sieve into a large saucepan and set aside, discarding the solids.

PREPARE THE PASTA: Remove the dough from the fridge. Using a pasta machine, or rolling by hand, roll the pasta to about the thickness of a toonie (about setting 4 on a pasta machine). We cut our dough into pappardelle for this recipe by simply cutting the sheets into 1-inch-wide pieces. Let the noodles rest for about 10 minutes to firm up.

Bring a large pot of salted water to boil. Cook the noodles in the boiling water for 3 to 4 minutes, then drain.

Continued

COMBINE EVERYTHING: Place the large saucepan with the sauce over medium heat and bring to a boil, stirring constantly. Once large bubbles form in the sauce, add the Parmesan and a pinch of salt. Stir well to combine.

Add the lobster meat to the sauce, then the cooked noodles. The starch from the pasta will thicken the sauce. Let simmer until the sauce thickens to your liking. Transfer to serving bowls and top with the green onions. Voila.

Dépanneur Surprise

Fred Morin

❝ It could be the gas station, the corner store, or the Plateau dépanneur (in Quebec), but it's the spot that's your last resort to feed your picky brood, short of tepid food delivered via tepid car. You've already failed by not achieving the proper meal planning for the evening, and you don't have enough fermenting crocks in the cellar to sustain the gang (I'm not sure if this has ever happened to you, but I can tell you, it definitely has happened to me).

Option one, which I do not suggest unless you are in an emergency parenting situation: you can pick up white bread and Doritos and make Doritos sandwiches, which may win you some major points with the kids but is guaranteed to lose you major points with your partner.

Option two, here's the thing: your local store definitely holds more gems on its shelves than you might expect. This ramen dish in its initial iteration kept popping up on the neighbouring table at our local Korean joint, a bubbling hot seafood stew, two standing monoliths of generic ramen, and a few slices of bright orange, plastic cheese (American processed). If you look into it, Roi Choi did a version a few years ago, but the recipe really dates back to when American soldiers were stationed in Korea. This version, using typical corner store—or dépanneur—ingredients and made up of ramen, some soup, and unassuming canned seafood, is actually delicious for the adult palate but is mostly for the kids. Don't knock it until you have no choice but to try it. ❞

SERVES 4
PREP TIME: 10 minutes
COOK TIME: 15 minutes

2 (284 ml/9.6 oz) cans tomato soup

Milk or water, to prepare the tomato soup according to package instructions

1 (115 g/4 oz) can small shrimp, drained

1 (120 g/4.25 oz) can crab meat, drained

2 (85 g/3 oz) packages dried ramen noodles (vegetable flavour, if possible)

4 slices American processed "cheese"

Sriracha, to taste

Salt and pepper, to taste

In a medium saucepan, heat the tomato soup. Add the shrimp and crab meat.

Warm a large serving bowl. Add the soup to the bowl. Place the two blocks of ramen noodles in the soup bowl so they are standing up, side by side, in the middle of the bowl.

Drape the cheese slices over the noodles and sprinkle one of the seasoning packets that came with the ramen over the soup. Keep the other packet for seasoning to taste.

Submerge the ramen blocks in the soup and let them sit until fully cooked. Mix the noodles and cheese carefully so they intermingle. Place the bowl ceremoniously in the centre of the table and appreciate the fact that you and your kids are about to sacrilegiously ingest cheese and seafood.

Baked Fish & Sweet Potato Chips

Joanna Fox

“ I know it's totally wrong, but I tell my son these are chicken fingers—and he eats them. I do think he's slightly suspicious, but that doesn't seem to stop him. I serve them to him with the ultimate honey-mustard dipping sauce, which is also wrong, but it kind of seals the deal in terms of legitimizing my whole ruse. ”

SERVES 4
PREP TIME: 30 minutes
COOK TIME: 40 minutes

SWEET POTATO CHIPS

2 sweet potatoes, peeled and cut into strips

1 tbsp olive oil

Salt and pepper, to taste

BAKED FISH

500 g (1.1 lb) cod or haddock

Salt and pepper

½ cup panko breadcrumbs

½ cup breadcrumbs

1 cup all-purpose flour

2 eggs, beaten

HONEY-MUSTARD DIPPING SAUCE

½ cup mayonnaise

¼ cup yellow mustard

¼ cup honey

Preheat the oven to 350°F.

MAKE THE SWEET POTATO CHIPS: In a bowl, toss the sweet potatoes with the oil, and salt and pepper, then transfer to a baking sheet. Bake for about 40 minutes, until golden and crispy.

MEANWHILE, MAKE THE BAKED FISH: Cut the fish into strips and season with salt and pepper. Place a metal rack over a parchment-paper-lined baking sheet. Mix the panko and breadcrumbs in a bowl, put the flour in another bowl, and the beaten eggs in a third bowl. Dredge the fish pieces first in the flour, then the eggs, then the breadcrumbs, and place them on the rack. Bake in the oven with the sweet potatoes for 25 minutes, or until golden.

MAKE THE HONEY-MUSTARD DIPPING SAUCE: Meanwhile, prepare the sauce by whisking all the ingredients together in a bowl.

Serve the fish and sweet potato chips with the honey-mustard dipping sauce.

Fish with Bran

Maha Barsoom

❝ This is a traditional way of grilling fish in Egypt, and it's very easy, healthy, and delicious! We coat the fish with bran before grilling to allow it to cook while keeping it moist inside. We do not eat the bran, we just peel the skin off with it, but it gives a great flavour to the fish. ❞

SERVES 6

PREP TIME: 20 minutes + 2 hours marinating

COOK TIME: 12 minutes

¼ cup white vinegar

1 large fish (tilapia, mullet, or sea bass), cleaned and rinsed

3 cloves garlic, minced

½ tsp ground cumin

½ tsp sea salt

½ tsp pepper

¼ tsp crushed red pepper flakes

Juice of 1 lemon

1 cup wheat bran

SAUCE

¼ cup white vinegar

1 clove garlic, minced

¼ tsp ground cumin

¼ tsp crushed red pepper flakes

Salt and pepper, to taste

Cooked rice, to serve

PREPARE THE FISH: Using the vinegar, rinse the insides of the fish thoroughly. Make three deep cuts on each side of the fish.

In a small bowl, combine the garlic, cumin, salt, pepper, red pepper flakes, and lemon juice. Mix to combine. Rub the spice mixture all over the fish, including the inside and the cuts. Transfer the fish to a container and place in the fridge. Let marinate for 2 hours.

COOK THE FISH: Heat your broiler to high. Line a baking sheet with parchment paper. Remove the fish from the fridge and thoroughly coat it with the bran. Place the fish on the prepared baking sheet. Broil the fish for about 6 minutes per side, or until the bran is charred.

MAKE THE SAUCE: Meanwhile, in a small bowl, combine all the ingredients for the sauce.

TO SERVE: When the fish is cooked, right before serving, peel the skin off, along with the bran. Debone the fish and portion it out, making sure the little ones don't get any bones. Drizzle with the sauce and serve hot with rice.

Roasted Salmon

Mandy Wolfe

❝ This recipe is constantly on rotation at our home, and the whole family adores it. ❞

SERVES 4 TO 6

PREP TIME: 5 minutes
    + 6 to 24 hours marinating
COOK TIME: 10 to 12 minutes

¾ cup tamari or soy sauce

¾ cup lightly packed brown sugar

1 tbsp toasted sesame oil

1 tbsp freshly squeezed
    orange juice

1 tsp grated fresh ginger

4 to 6 salmon filets

Cooked jasmine rice, to serve

Toasted sesame seeds, to serve
    (optional)

Sliced green onions, to serve
    (optional)

In a medium bowl, whisk together the tamari or soy sauce, sugar, oil, orange juice, and ginger. Add the salmon filets and toss to fully coat them in the marinade. Place the filets in a sealable dish or bag and let marinate in the fridge for a few hours, or up to 24 hours. The longer it sits, the tastier it will be.

Preheat the oven to 450°F. Line a baking sheet with parchment paper. Place the filets on the prepared sheet, skin-side down. Top with any extra marinade left in the bag and place in the top third of the oven. Bake for 10 to 12 minutes, with the last 2 to 3 minutes on broil to caramelize the sugar. Cook for a bit longer if you prefer the salmon completely opaque.

Serve with fluffy jasmine rice, topped with toasted sesame seeds and green onions.

Roast Chicken with Ginger & Green Onion

Brian Ng

" I grew up with two Chinese immigrant parents in a small town in Yukon Territory, and I was regularly exposed to my mother's incredible Cantonese home cooking of the dishes she grew up eating, including a poached whole chicken with ginger and green onion sauce. In Canada, though, roast chicken seemed to me to be the ultimate home comfort food that you would cook for your family, and I was always a little envious when my friends' parents were preparing one when I was at their houses playing, because we never ate roast chicken at our house. I eventually learned to cook one myself, using Julia Child's recipe, at the ripe young age of 14. And so this recipe is a sort of mélange: my Chinese upbringing in Canada, a twist on an old recipe that you will find in most Asian households, the classic Canadian roast chicken dinner, and Julia Child's perfect roast chicken recipe. Although I don't have kids of my own, this recipe reminds me of when I was a kid. This is, and always will be, a kid favourite—just ask my 10-year-old niece (with whom I always fight for the drumsticks). **"**

SERVES 4 TO 6

PREP TIME: 20 minutes + 1 hour resting

COOK TIME: 1 hour 10 minutes

1 whole chicken
(about 1.1 kg/2.5 lb)

Salt

Ground white pepper

1 lemon, halved

1 bunch green onions, green parts minced (for the Sauce, below) and white parts left whole

¼ cup butter, at room temperature

4 cups jasmine rice

5 cups water

SAUCE

2-inch piece fresh ginger, finely minced

2 cloves garlic, minced

2 tbsp finely chopped cilantro stems (optional)

½ cup canola, sunflower, or grapeseed oil

Preheat the oven to 350°F.

PREPARE AND COOK THE CHICKEN: Pat the chicken dry with paper towels and leave at room temperature for 1 hour. Season the chicken liberally, outside and inside, with salt and white pepper. Stuff the cavity with the lemon halves and white parts of the green onions. Using butcher's twine, tie the drumsticks together and tuck the wings under the chicken. Using your hands, massage the chicken with the butter and place the chicken on a roasting rack set over a baking pan.

Roast the chicken for 55 minutes. Raise the oven temperature to 425°F and continue roasting for another 15 minutes to crisp up the skin. The chicken should be fully cooked. Remove the chicken from the oven and let rest for 20 minutes before carving.

MEANWHILE, MAKE THE RICE: Rinse the rice in several changes of water until it is no longer cloudy. Strain and place in your favourite rice cooker. Add the 5 cups of water and cook the rice according to the manufacturer's instructions.

MAKE THE SAUCE: In a medium bowl, combine the minced green onions, ginger, garlic, cilantro stems, and salt and pepper to taste. Heat the oil in a small pot until almost smoking, then carefully ladle the hot oil over the onion mixture, a little at a time, stirring after each addition.

TO SERVE: Serve the chicken, sliced, with the rice, green onion sauce, and any leftover sautéed greens you might have in the fridge.

Lemongrass Chicken

Alex Chen

> **This is a pretty healthy recipe, with a lot of hidden vegetables and herbs. I like making it for my family because not only is it delicious, but we can all enjoy it together too.**

SERVES 4 TO 6

PREP TIME: 30 minutes + overnight marinating

COOK TIME: 20 minutes

2 stalks lemongrass, inner tender stalks finely minced

3 tbsp grated garlic

1 tbsp fish sauce

½ tbsp oyster sauce

1 kg (2.2 lb) boneless, skinless chicken thighs, cubed

Bamboo skewers (soaked in water)

NOODLES & GARNISHES

½ package Vietnamese pho rice noodles

2 medium carrots, julienned

1 small red onion, halved, thinly sliced

1 Japanese cucumber, sliced

¼ cup chopped cilantro leaves

¼ cup chopped mint leaves

½ cup roasted peanuts, coarsely chopped

DRESSING

⅔ cup water

⅓ cup fish sauce

¼ cup lime juice

¼ cup sugar

3 tbsp Thai sweet chili sauce

Zest of ½ lime

Pepper, to taste

MARINADE THE CHICKEN: In a medium bowl, mix the lemongrass, garlic, fish sauce, and oyster sauce together. Add the chicken, cover, and let marinate overnight in the fridge.

MAKE THE NOODLES & GARNISHES: Place the red onion in a bowl of ice water and let soak for 1 hour. Place the carrots in a separate bowl of ice water and let soak for 30 minutes. Bring a medium pot of water to a boil. Add the rice noodles and cook for 6 minutes. (I like my noodles cooked through.) Strain the noodles, then place them in a bowl of cold water for 5 minutes. Strain again and let dry for 15 minutes. Drain the julienned carrots and red onions.

MAKE THE DRESSING: In a small bowl, whisk all the ingredients together until the sugar dissolves. Season to taste with pepper.

GRILL THE CHICKEN: When ready, thread the chicken onto bamboo skewers. Over a charcoal or gas grill set on medium heat, grill the skewers until the chicken reaches an internal temperature of 160°F, about 7 minutes. Remove from the heat. Once cool enough to handle, remove the chicken from the skewers.

TO SERVE: Divide the rice noodles between the serving bowls. Top with the vegetables and chicken and drizzle with the lime dressing. Top with the chopped herbs and peanuts.

Saffron Chicken with Parmesan Pudding

Derek Dammann

❝ This is my version of a simple chicken-with-green-vegetable dinner. Turns out my son loves saffron, so I added that in a marinade for the chicken and in the butter to finish the veggies. You could add whatever green veg you fancy; asparagus or green beans would be lovely too. The bonus is that everything uses the same pan in the end (aside from the pudding), so a big win when it comes to the cleanup. ❞

SERVES 4 TO 6

PREP TIME: 40 minutes + overnight marinating

COOK TIME: 1½ hours

CHICKEN & VEGETABLES

1 tsp saffron threads

4 tbsp olive oil

3 tbsp butter, at room temperature

6 boneless, skin-on chicken breasts

2 tbsp chopped flat-leaf parsley

1 tbsp finely chopped fresh thyme leaves

Zest and juice of 1 lemon

Salt and pepper, to taste

340 g (¾ lb) sugar snap peas, sliced on the diagonal into ¼-inch pieces

1½ cups green onions, thinly sliced, white and green parts separated

1 tbsp water

115 g (4 oz) pea shoots

Continued

PREPARE THE CHICKEN: In a small pan over medium heat, toast the saffron. Transfer to a mortar and pestle and grind to a fine powder. Remove half of the saffron to a small bowl and mix with 3 tablespoons of the oil. Mix the remaining saffron with 1 tablespoon of the butter and stir with a rubber spatula until well combined. Set aside.

In a large bowl, combine the chicken breasts with the saffron oil, half of the parsley, 2 teaspoons of the thyme, and the lemon zest. Toss until well mixed, cover, and let marinate in the fridge overnight.

Remove the chicken from the fridge 1 hour before cooking so it can come to room temperature.

MAKE THE PUDDING: Preheat the oven to 350°F. Butter a 6 × 8-inch baking dish and set aside.

In a medium pot over medium heat, heat the butter. When it begins to foam, whisk in the flour, 1 tablespoon at a time, and cook for 5 minutes, whisking all the while to prevent the flour from scorching. You do not want the flour to brown. Slowly add the milk and cream, whisking constantly until smooth. Continue cooking the mixture for a few minutes, whisking constantly, until it is smooth and starts to simmer.

In a small bowl, whisk the eggs and egg yolks together. Slowly drizzle them into the cream mixture, whisking constantly until fully incorporated. Add the Parmesan and season to taste with salt and pepper.

Pour the mixture into the prepared baking dish and cover tightly with aluminum foil. Place the baking dish in a deep roasting pan and add enough hot water to come halfway up the sides of the dish. Bake for about 1 hour, until the pudding is just set.

Continued

PUDDING

3 tbsp butter

6 tbsp all-purpose flour

1¾ cups milk

⅔ cup heavy cream

2 eggs

2 egg yolks

1¼ cups grated Parmesan

Salt and pepper, to taste

COOK THE CHICKEN & VEGETABLES: In a large sauté pan over medium heat, heat the remaining 1 tablespoon of olive oil. Season the chicken on both sides with salt and pepper and place in the pan skin-side down. You might have to work in batches, adding more oil as needed. Sauté until the skin is golden brown and crispy about 5 to 7 minutes. Flip the chicken and reduce the heat to medium-low. Cook until the chicken breasts are cooked through and springy to the touch, another 5 to 7 minutes. Transfer the chicken to a cooling rack.

Using the same pan over medium heat, add the remaining 2 tablespoons of butter. As soon as it begins to foam, add the sugar snap peas and the white parts of the green onions. Season with ½ teaspoon salt, a pinch of pepper, and the remaining thyme. Cook for 2 to 3 minutes, stirring occasionally with a wooden spoon, until the onions are translucent.

Add the saffron butter and 1 tablespoon of water. Swirl the pan and bring to a simmer. Add the pea shoots and green onion tops. Immediately remove from the heat and add the lemon juice. Taste and adjust the seasoning as needed.

TO SERVE: Place the chicken on a large, warm platter, spoon the vegetables over top, and serve with the pudding. Garnish with the remaining parsley.

Chicken Enchiladas

Nick Hodge

❝ Enchiladas are sort of like Tex-Mex lasagna. Sort of. My girls love them because they're delicious, fun to eat, and a good way to get the whole family involved—my advice is to set up an assembly line. And make a big batch! They freeze really well uncooked. The condiments I've included recipes for are always found in our fridge. They're super easy to make, even in large quantities—which I suggest you do, as they are so versatile! Add them to salads or sandwiches, use them to garnish other dishes, or snack on them chips 'n' dip style. ❞

SERVES 4
PREP TIME: 30 minutes
COOK TIME: 40 minutes

CHICKEN ENCHILADAS

¼ cup canola oil

16 corn tortillas

2 cups chicken broth

4 tomatoes, coarsely chopped

3 tomatillos, coarsely chopped

1 Spanish onion, diced

3 cloves garlic

Salt and pepper, to taste

2 guajillo chilies

2 mulato chilies

1 rotisserie chicken, shredded

½ onion, finely diced

3 cups shredded cheddar or
   Monterey Jack

Condiments of choice
   (see page 156), to serve

Continued

MAKE THE CHICKEN ENCHILADAS: In a skillet over medium-high heat, heat the oil. Fry 14 of the tortillas, one at a time, until golden. Set aside.

In a medium saucepan, combine the broth, tomatoes, tomatillos, Spanish onions, garlic, and the remaining two tortillas. Bring to a boil then reduce the heat and simmer until ready to use. Season to taste.

Preheat the oven to 350°F. Place all the chilies on a small baking sheet and bake for 5 minutes. When they are cool enough to handle, remove the stems and seeds. Add them to the broth and cook for 10 minutes. Remove the sauce from the heat and blend in a blender or with an immersion blender until smooth. Pour the sauce into a shallow dish.

Dip the fried tortillas in the sauce, then fill them with the chicken, onions, and some of the cheese, and roll them up. Place them in a rectangular casserole dish. Continue rolling the tortillas until they are all filled, cover them with a layer of the remaining sauce, and sprinkle with the remaining cheese. Bake for 15 to 20 minutes until the cheese has browned and the contents are bubbling on the sides. Meanwhile, prepare your chosen condiments (see the next page).

TO SERVE: Serve the condiments in an assembly line of bowls, let your family pick their favourites, and use them to top their hot enchiladas.

Continued

PICKLED RED ONIONS

2 red onions, julienned

½ cup sugar

2 cups apple cider vinegar

Salt and pepper, to taste

PICO DE GALLO

1 cup chopped tomatoes

2 jalapeños, seeded and diced

½ onion, diced

1 clove garlic, minced

Juice of 3 limes

Salt and pepper, to taste

CHIPOTLE MAYO

2 canned chipotle peppers
   in adobo sauce

2 cups mayonnaise

RANCH DRESSING

2 cloves garlic, finely minced

⅓ cup finely chopped chives

½ Spanish onion, finely chopped

3 cups mayonnaise

¾ cup buttermilk

1 tbsp Dijon mustard

Salt and pepper, to taste

FOR THE PICKLED RED ONIONS: In a medium pot, combine all the ingredients and bring to a boil. Simmer for 5 minutes, then remove from the heat and let cool to room temperature before refrigerating. Store in an airtight container in the fridge for up to 1 week.

FOR THE PICO DE GALLO: In a small bowl, combine all the ingredients and mix to combine. Season to taste and store in an airtight container in the fridge for up to 1 week.

FOR THE CHIPOTLE MAYO: In a blender, blend the chipotle and mayonnaise together until smooth. Store in an airtight container in the fridge for up to 1 week.

FOR THE RANCH DRESSING: In a medium bowl, whisk together all the ingredients until combined. Store in an airtight container in the fridge for up to 1 week.

Chicken Brochettes

Joanna Fox

❝ When I was a kid, my parents would take me and my sister to a particular bring-your-own-wine restaurant in Montreal. They loved it because it was always bustling, the food was good, the place was super family-friendly, and the price was right for the wine. My sister and I loved it because we got to go out to eat, which made us feel grown-up and special. We would always order chicken brochettes and get these heaping plates filled with plump, juicy chicken, rice, potatoes, and salad (which, of course, I didn't eat until later in life). And when I had my son, this was also one of his first restaurant experiences, and I'm sure you can guess what he ate. This recipe is basically my take on the flavours I remember eating as a kid, and it's a staple in our weekly rotation. I can safely say that it will please the picky eaters as well as the adults. I like to serve this to my son with hummus (only because he does not like tzatziki or yogurt—the joy!), fresh pita, cucumber slices, and homemade oven fries. I, on the other hand, love it with salad. **❞**

SERVES 4 TO 6

PREP TIME: 15 minutes + at least 4 hours or overnight marinating

COOK TIME: 25 minutes

8 chicken thighs or 4 boneless skinless chicken breasts, cubed

2 tbsp olive oil

1 tbsp lemon juice

1 tbsp plain yogurt

1 tbsp honey

1 tsp Dijon mustard

1 to 2 cloves garlic, finely grated

1 tsp salt

½ tsp pepper

4 to 6 metal or wood skewers (latter soaked in water)

Place the cubed chicken in a medium bowl. In a small bowl, whisk together the remaining ingredients to make a marinade. Pour the marinade over the chicken and mix well to combine. Cover the bowl with plastic wrap or a lid and let marinate in the fridge for at least 4 hours, and preferably overnight.

Turn on the barbecue to medium heat and oil the grill. Thread the cubed chicken onto the skewers (discard any remaining marinade) and place on the hot grill. Cook for about 25 minutes (turn halfway through cooking) until cooked through. Serve with your choice of rice, potatoes, salad, pita, and dips.

NOTE: Feel free to use this marinade on any meat you like. Although I prefer to grill the brochettes on the barbecue, Canadian winters might mean you'd prefer to bake them in the oven (about 30 minutes at 350°F).

Cheesy Chicken Katsu

Ryusuke Nakagawa

66 As the executive chef for the upscale Aburi Hana, I'm used to cooking for some of the most discerning palates in the world with some of the finest ingredients available. But the most VIP diner to me is my daughter. As any parent knows, young kids can be the most challenging to cook for, and my daughter is no exception. It took a lot of experimenting and a lot of rejected dishes, but I finally found the one thing that she'll happily devour. She was okay with the original katsu I made her, but once I added cheese into the recipe, that definitely hit a home run with her. It's crunchy on the outside and soft and juicy on the inside, and the gooey cheese adds just the right balance of chewy. 99

SERVES 4
PREP TIME: 10 minutes
COOK TIME: 7 minutes

4 boneless, skinless chicken breasts, butterflied

8 whole umeboshi (preserved Japanese plums), pitted

Salt and pepper, to taste

8 shiso leaves

1 cup shredded mozzarella

Canola oil, for frying

1 cup all-purpose flour

2 eggs

2 cups panko breadcrumbs

1 cup minced daikon

⅓ cup ponzu sauce

Cooked rice, for serving

Using a tenderizer or mallet, flatten the chicken breasts until they are wide and thin.

Mince the umeboshi plums until they are reduced to a paste. Season the chicken with salt and pepper on both sides. Place the shiso leaves, cheese, and umeboshi paste in the centre of each breast and fold over to encase the filling.

In a small, deep skillet, add the oil (deep enough to cover at least half the chicken) and heat to 350°F.

Place the flour on a shallow plate. Whisk the eggs in a medium bowl. Place the panko on another plate. Dredge the chicken first in the flour, then the eggs, and finally the panko.

Fry the chicken for about 7 minutes, turning during cooking, until the breadcrumbs are golden brown and the chicken is cooked through. Remove the chicken from the oil and place on a paper-towel-lined plate to rest for 1 minute and absorb excess oil. Slice into even pieces, easy for a child to eat.

In another bowl, combine the daikon and ponzu. Drizzle this over the chicken or plate in a bowl on the side, and serve with rice.

Butter Chicken Schnitzel

Vikram Vij

" This is a recipe I created for my daughters, Nanaki and Shanik, and it became a regular indulgence in our home. We basically took breaded chicken and rich, creamy butter chicken sauce and put them together for what ended up being an amazing recipe and what is now our signature family dish. **"**

SERVES 6
PREP TIME: 25 minutes
COOK TIME: 20 minutes

SAUCE

⅓ cup vegetable oil

1 small onion, finely chopped

1 head garlic, peeled and crushed (about 2 to 3 tbsp)

1 small can tomato paste or ¾ cup crushed tomatoes

1 tbsp paprika

2 tsp ground cumin

1½ tsp salt

1 tsp ground turmeric

1 tsp ground coriander

1½ cups water

1½ cups heavy cream

CHICKEN

900 g (2 lb) boneless, skinless chicken breasts or thighs

½ cup all-purpose flour

1 tsp salt

2 eggs

1 cup dried breadcrumbs

½ cup vegetable oil, for frying

MAKE THE SAUCE: In a medium pot, heat the oil over medium heat. Add the onions and sauté for 3 to 4 minutes, or until lightly golden. Add the garlic and sauté for 1 minute. Reduce the heat to low and add the tomato paste, stirring well.

Add the paprika, cumin, salt, turmeric, and coriander. Stir well and sauté for 4 minutes. Add the water and cream and stir to combine. Remove the sauce from the heat and set aside until ready to serve.

MAKE THE CHICKEN: Lay out the pieces of chicken on a cutting board and lightly pound them with the heel of your hand to flatten them. Place the flour and salt in a shallow plate and mix to combine. Place the eggs in a medium bowl and whisk until homogeneous. Place the breadcrumbs in another shallow plate.

Dredge the chicken in the flour until lightly coated. Transfer the chicken to the eggs, and coat all sides. Transfer to the breadcrumbs and press to adhere on all sides. Place the chicken on a baking sheet.

In a large frying pan, heat the oil over medium-high heat. Once the oil is hot, add the chicken pieces and fry until golden brown and fully cooked through, about 3 minutes per side. Transfer the chicken to a paper-towel-lined baking sheet to absorb excess oil.

TO SERVE: Bring the sauce to a boil. Reduce the heat and simmer for 5 minutes. Remove from the heat. Serve the chicken with the sauce in small bowls alongside for dipping.

My Favourite Childhood Chicken

Susur Lee

" I love this recipe because it reminds me of growing up and eating street food in Hong Kong. It's easy enough to make with your kids, or for them, after a long day. The recipe fuses a variety of cultures and lends itself well to one of the most versatile proteins in the world. My kids and their friends loved it growing up. Sometimes, when I'm feeling nostalgic, I make it just for my wife and me. **"**

SERVES 4
PREP TIME: 10 minutes + marinating
COOK TIME: 20 minutes

CHICKEN

4 boneless, skinless chicken thighs, cut into fingers or bite-sized pieces

1 tsp grated fresh ginger

¼ tsp Chinese five spice

¼ cup olive oil

3 tbsp cornstarch

SAUCE

¼ cup chicken stock

2 tbsp ketchup

1 tbsp soy sauce

Crushed red pepper flakes (optional)

MAKE THE CHICKEN: In a medium bowl, combine the chicken pieces with the ginger and five spice and let marinate in the fridge for at least 30 minutes and up to 3 hours.

In a medium frying pan over medium heat, heat the oil.

Working in batches, dust the chicken pieces with the cornstarch, shaking off the excess, and fry in the oil until crispy, about 3 to 4 minutes per side. Repeat until all the chicken pieces are fried.

MAKE THE SAUCE: In a small bowl, combine the stock, ketchup, and soy sauce, adjusting to taste. A little crushed red pepper flakes can also be added, if desired. Pour the sauce over the chicken, or into a bowl to serve on the side, and serve with rice or your favourite side dish.

BBQ Turkey Burgers

Robin Wasicuna

> My daughter, Gabrielle, and I have been eating burgers together since she was old enough to eat solid food. My love for burgers was definitely passed down to her! We've eaten many over the years, and as we've get older, healthier eating has taken precedence. Here is our recipe for lean turkey burgers. We hope you enjoy them as much as we do!

MAKES 4 BURGERS
PREP TIME: 20 minutes
COOK TIME: 10 minutes

BURGERS

2 strips bacon

454 g (1 lb) ground turkey

1 tsp salt

1 tsp pepper

BBQ SAUCE

½ cup ketchup

¼ cup yellow mustard

¼ cup apple cider vinegar

1 tbsp Worcestershire sauce

1 tbsp liquid smoke

1 tsp honey

2 tbsp dried oregano

1 tbsp garlic powder

1½ tsp salt

1½ tsp pepper

TO SERVE

4 burger buns, toasted

¼ red onion, thinly sliced

1 avocado, thinly sliced

MAKE THE BURGERS: In a food processor, pulse the bacon until it forms a paste. Transfer the bacon to a medium bowl. Add the ground turkey, salt, and pepper and mix until the mixture is homogeneous. Divide into eight balls and flatten into patties ¼-inch thick.

MAKE THE BBQ SAUCE: In a medium bowl, combine all the ingredients and mix until combined. Store in an airtight container in the fridge for up to 2 weeks, or the freezer for up to 3 months.

COOK THE BURGERS AND SERVE: In a skillet over medium heat, cook the burgers until they are fully cooked through and firm, about 4 minutes each side. Place a dollop of the BBQ sauce on the bottom half of the bun, followed by the red onion slices. Top with the burger, avocado, and the top half of the bun and serve.

Frybread Stuffed Pizza

Billy Alexander

❝ My daughter and I have a lot of fun together making this pizza from scratch, and it gives us time to bond. I get to observe her as she goes through each step of the recipe with me, and I'm constantly surprised and fascinated by how incredibly complex and astute this little person is. You can learn a lot about a person by just watching how they handle themselves in the kitchen. It also makes me happy that she likes frybread versus the typical pizza dough. I try to fold some of our Indigenous roots into whatever we make at home. **❞**

MAKES 6 TO 8 PIZZA POCKETS
PREP TIME: 20 minutes
COOK TIME: 24 to 32 minutes

3 cups all-purpose flour,
    plus more for dusting

1 tbsp baking powder

½ tsp salt

1½ cups warm water

2 cups pizza sauce

40 pieces mini pepperoni

454 g (1 lb) mozzarella, shredded

3 cups vegetable oil

In a large bowl, combine the flour, baking powder, and salt and mix until combined. Make a small well in the middle of the flour mixture and add the warm water. Gently fold the flour mixture into the water, using a light touch, until the dough is completely homogeneous. Do not overmix the dough, as this will make it dense and heavy.

Place the dough on a lightly floured work surface and lightly knead it. Divide it into six to eight pieces, depending on the size you want. Roll each piece into a circle ¼-inch thick and make a small depression using your thumb in the centre of each.

Spread some pizza sauce over the surface of each circle. Add some pepperoni, about five to six pieces for each, and a small mound of mozzarella. Fold over one edge of the dough overtop of the filling and seal the edges together.

In a large cast-iron skillet, heat the oil until it reaches 350°F. Working in batches, carefully transfer the frybread to the oil and fry until each side is puffed up and golden, about 2 minutes per side. Transfer the frybreads to a paper-towel-lined plate to absorb excess oil, then keep warm on a baking sheet in the oven at 250°F. Continue frying the remaining breads.

Serve whole or cut in halves with any extra pizza sauce for dipping. Store in an airtight container in the fridge for up to 3 days.

Duck Empanadas

Ari Schor

> 66 Empanadas always make me think of my parents' home. They seem to magically appear when we come over to visit. I learned to make them there as well. There's nothing like your dad schooling you on making the repulgue (the traditional braided fold for the edge of the empanada), then roasting you when you fall behind. These are perfect for kids because they're small and easy to eat—as an appetizer for the adults and a main for the little ones.
>
> This recipe is for the first version of the empanadas that we served at Beba, the restaurant I run in Montreal with my brother, Pablo. It's a nod to the local duck producers in the province and a sort of Frenchy, hoity-toity variation on the classic versions you find back home in Argentina. The chopped egg and olive are essential; duck and olives are a classic pairing, and then there's the fact ducks lay eggs. It works. You know it works. Sometimes confit duck gizzards make it in there too. 99

MAKES 12 EMPANADAS; SERVES 6
PREP TIME: 1 hour + overnight resting
COOK TIME: 1 hour 35 minutes

FILLING

¼ cup olive oil

2½ cups ground duck
(about 500 g/1.1 lb) (see Note)

3 cups diced onions

4 cloves garlic, minced

1 tbsp sweet paprika

1 tbsp salt

1 tsp pepper

¼ cup red wine

2 cups chicken stock (or duck
stock, if you want to be a nerd)

4 hard-boiled eggs, peeled and
coarsely chopped

½ cup pitted green olives,
coarsely chopped (use the best
green olives you can find and
pit them yourself)

Continued

MAKE THE FILLING: In a large, wide pot, heat the oil over medium-high heat. Add the duck meat and brown, stirring with a wooden spoon. Turn the heat down to medium and add the onions. Cook until meltingly tender, stirring occasionally, about 10 minutes.

Add the garlic, paprika, salt, and pepper and cook for 4 minutes. Add the wine and stock and stir to dislodge any pieces stuck to the bottom of the pot.

Turn the heat down to low and cook, covered, for at least 1 hour, or until the liquid has reduced and the meat is tender. It should look thick and rich, like a ragu. Remove from the heat and let cool. Add the eggs and olives and fold to combine. Cover and refrigerate overnight.

MEANWHILE, MAKE THE DOUGH: In a medium bowl, combine the flour and salt. Add the duck fat and work the mixture until it resembles coarse sand. Add the water all at once and mix until just combined.

On a clean work surface, knead the dough until it is stretchy and uniform, about 5 minutes. Wrap the dough in plastic wrap and refrigerate overnight.

TO ASSEMBLE: Bring the dough to room temperature for an hour before rolling. Preheat the oven to 450°F. Line a baking sheet with parchment paper or aluminum foil.

On a lightly floured work surface, roll out the dough to ⅛-inch thick using a rolling pin or wine bottle. Cut out twelve 5-inch circles. I use the lip of a cereal bowl as a guide and a butter knife to cut the dough.

Lay the dough circles on a clean work surface. Place ¼ cup of the cold filling in each. Brush one half of the dough edge with a bit of water. Fold the circles in half and press the edges together.

Continued

DOUGH

3 cups all-purpose flour

2 tsp salt

½ cup duck fat

¾ cup cold water

1 egg, beaten

1 tbsp milk

Crimp the edges with a fork or follow an online tutorial for the culturally appropriate repulgue. Place the empanadas on the prepared baking sheet.

In a small bowl, whisk together the egg and milk. Using a pastry brush, glaze the tops of the empanadas with the egg wash.

Bake for 20 minutes, turning the baking sheet halfway through the cooking time. The empanadas should be nicely browned. Feast! Store in an airtight container in the fridge for up to 1 week or the freezer for up to 3 months.

NOTE: Ask your butcher for ground duck, preferably a mix of leg and heart. If you don't eat duck, don't make this recipe. In fact, we can't be friends.

Ramen Carbonara

Suzanne Barr

66 My son, like most kids, enjoys eating things that have some familiarity, and this ramen carbonara is one of his favourites: it combines easy instant noodles with the comforting taste of butter and bacon. For him, it's like having a taste of Japan and Italy in one bowl, and he polishes it off every single time I make it for him. 99

SERVES 4
PREP TIME: 5 minutes
COOK TIME: 20 minutes

8 strips bacon, cut into ¼-inch pieces

4 (85 g/3 oz) packages dried ramen noodles

¼ cup butter

½ cup soy sauce

½ cup hoisin sauce

1 cup English peas, cooked

In a medium skillet over medium heat, cook the bacon until the fat is rendered and the meat is cooked through. Turn down the heat if necessary to prevent scorching. Using a slotted spoon, transfer the bacon to a paper-towel-lined plate to absorb excess oil. Set aside.

Remove the bacon fat from the pan (reserve for another use, if desired) and leave any brown bits stuck to the pan.

Meanwhile, bring a large pot of water to a boil. Add the ramen noodles and cook until soft, about 3 to 4 minutes. Drain and set aside.

Return the bacon skillet to medium-high heat and add the butter and the noodles. Scrape any browned bits from the bottom of the pan into the butter, and toss to coat the noodles.

Add the soy sauce and hoisin sauce, turn the heat to high, and stir constantly as the sauce thickens. Reduce the heat to low, mix in the bacon and peas, and remove from the heat. Serve immediately.

Tonnarelli with Sunday Gravy

Danny Smiles

66 Italians love their Sunday sauces, or what I like to call a Sunday gravy. It's basically a tomato sauce that you cook meat in, but then you take the meat out to serve separately and toss the sauce with pasta. When I put this on the table, my son Lennon literally squeals with delight. He's always reaching to grab the biggest rib or piece of meat. I mean, I'm not surprised that my kid loves to eat. He's been around food and cooking his whole life, but the smile on his face when I serve this meal—it's priceless. 99

SERVES 4 TO 6
PREP TIME: 10 minutes
COOK TIME: 2½ hours

3 tbsp olive oil, plus more to serve

1 rack pork ribs, cut into 3 pieces
    (I prefer Berkshire)

Salt and pepper, to taste

1 medium yellow onion, diced

2 cloves garlic, minced

4 mild Italian sausages

2 tbsp tomato paste

½ cup red wine

2 litres passata (crushed
    tomatoes)

1 (500 g/17.65 oz) package
    tonnarelli, or your favourite
    pasta

Grated Parmesan, to serve

Photos on pages 170 and 171

In a large enamelled pot over medium-high heat, heat the oil until shimmering. Season the pork ribs with salt and pepper and sear them in the pot until they are a beautiful golden brown, about 8 minutes. Remove the ribs from the pot and set aside.

In the same pot, cook the onions for 10 minutes, until they start to brown. Add the garlic and stir. Return the ribs to the pot along with the sausages, tomato paste, and wine.

Stir until the wine has evaporated, then add the passata. Simmer, partially covered, for about 2 hours.

When you are ready to serve, bring a large pot of salted water to a boil. Add the tonnarelli and cook until al dente. Drain the pasta, reserving a bit of the cooking liquid. Remove the ribs and sausages from the sauce and place them on a serving platter.

Add the pasta to the sauce and toss well, then add a splash of olive oil. Add some of the reserved cooking liquid if the sauce is too thick. Serve the pasta with the ribs and sausages alongside and top with some grated Parmesan. Buon appetito.

Braised Pork & Shiitake Meatballs

Anita Feng

SERVES 6
PREP TIME: 30 minutes
COOK TIME: 1 hour to 1 hour 10 minutes

MEATBALLS

600 g (1⅓ lb) minced pork (at least 30% fat)

¾ cup chopped fresh shiitake mushrooms

1 egg, lightly beaten

1 tbsp light soy sauce

1 tsp sesame oil

1 tbsp Shaoxing rice wine

1 tbsp cornstarch, plus more for dusting

½ tsp salt

¼ tsp sugar

1 green onion, coarsely chopped

1-inch piece fresh ginger, sliced into 4 pieces

⅓ cup water

2 cups canola oil, for frying

STOCK

1 cup vegetable or chicken stock or water

¼ cup light soy sauce

3 tbsp Shaoxing rice wine

2 tbsp sugar (ideally rock sugar)

1 dry bay leaf

1 cinnamon stick

1 star anise

Green onions, chopped, to garnish

Cilantro leaves, chopped, to garnish

Steamed rice, to serve

> 66 Some of my best childhood memories from growing up in China are the times I spent with my grandparents. This dish is my grandma's, who was not a prolific cook. She had only a couple of recipes, and we would have the same thing practically all the time. It sounds boring, right? But for me, my grandma was the best cook. All those dishes are engraved in my head, and whenever I think of her, I can almost feel and taste her dishes on my tongue. My dad and I tried to recreate this recipe so many times—but it never tasted like my grandma's. Here's my best version so far. 99

MAKE THE MEATBALLS: In a medium bowl, combine the pork, shiitakes, egg, soy sauce, sesame oil, rice wine, cornstarch, salt, and sugar and mix to combine.

In a small bowl, mix the green onions and ginger with the water and squeeze them until their juices release, about 3 minutes. Remove the onions and ginger and reserve for later.

Add the water to the meatball mixture and stir until all the liquid has been absorbed. Begin working the mixture vigorously until it becomes very sticky, about 5 minutes. Divide the mixture into six meatballs and dust them with the extra cornstarch. Set aside.

In a small pot, heat the oil to 265°F. Fry the meatballs one at a time until golden brown, about 3 to 5 minutes. Set the meatballs aside.

MAKE THE STOCK: In a large pot, add 1 tablespoon of the frying oil from the meatballs. Add the reserved onion and ginger pieces from the meatballs. Add the stock, soy sauce, rice wine, sugar, bay leaf, cinnamon, and star anise and bring to a boil. Add the meatballs, cover, turn down to a simmer, and cook for 40 minutes.

TO SERVE: Remove the meatballs from the stock and set on a serving platter. Remove any solids from the stock and discard them. Bring the stock to a boil and reduce until it forms a thick gravy. Pour the gravy over the meatballs and garnish with green onions and cilantro. Serve with steamed rice.

Photo on page 121

Tomato-Braised Sausages with Green Onion Purée

Jessica Noël

66 This was one of my favourite dinners that my mother used to make when I was a kid. It's quick and can be made into tons of variations with whatever you have at home. My mom often made this recipe with breakfast sausages, and it was delicious. I think pork and fennel sausages would be the best, but honestly most sausages could work. You can sneak in extra veggies, like roasted red peppers and fennel in the braise, and the purée could be combined with cauliflower or rutabaga as well. 99

SERVES 4 TO 6
PREP TIME: 20 minutes
COOK TIME: 30 minutes

SAUSAGES

2 tbsp olive oil

8 sausages of your choice

1 onion, chopped

2 cloves garlic, chopped

Pinch crushed red pepper flakes

Salt, to taste

½ cup red wine

1 small (443 ml/15 oz) can Italian
    tomatoes, crushed by hand

1 sprig rosemary

PURÉE

454 g (1 lb) Yukon Gold potatoes,
    peeled and cut into large cubes

½ cup milk

¼ cup butter, cut into small cubes

Salt and pepper, to taste

1 bunch green onions, sliced

COOK THE SAUSAGES: In a large skillet over medium-high heat, heat the oil. Add the sausages and brown them on all sides. You are not looking to fully cook them, but rather caramelize them. Remove the sausages from the pan and set aside.

In the same skillet, add the onions, garlic, red pepper flakes, and salt. Cook until the onions are translucent. Add the red wine and let simmer until reduced by half. Add the tomatoes, sausages, and rosemary. Bring to a simmer and cook, covered, over medium-low heat for about 15 minutes. Taste and adjust the seasoning as needed and serve with the purée.

MEANWHILE, MAKE THE PURÉE: Place the potatoes in a large pot and cover with cold water. Bring to a simmer over medium heat and cook the potatoes until tender, about 15 minutes.

In a small saucepan over medium heat, bring the milk to a simmer. Remove from the heat and set aside.

Once the potatoes are tender, drain them and place them in the bowl of a stand mixer. Using the paddle attachment, purée the potatoes while they are still very hot. Add the milk in a slow, steady stream with the mixer running on low.

Once the milk is incorporated, add the butter, one cube at a time. Make sure there are no lumps! Season to taste with salt and pepper. Fold in the green onions and serve with the sausages.

Pork Schnitzel

David McMillan

66 Kids love to eat things that are crispy and crunchy, and this recipe is great because you can make it with whatever protein you have on hand—chicken, pork, or veal. When I asked my three daughters which of the meals I make for them is their favourite, this one was right up there. Serve this with my Mandoline Vegetable Salad (page 66) on the side. **99**

SERVES 4
PREP TIME: 20 minutes
COOK TIME: 30 minutes

4 boneless pork chops, pounded thin (or use chicken breast or veal breast)

Salt and pepper, to taste

½ cup all-purpose flour

2 eggs, beaten

1 cup dried breadcrumbs

2 tsp dried sage

1 tsp garlic salt

1 tsp white pepper

Canola oil, for frying

1 lemon, quartered, to serve

Few sprigs flat-leaf parsley, to serve

Lightly season the pork chops with salt and pepper. Place the flour in a shallow bowl. Place the eggs in another shallow bowl. Place the breadcrumbs, sage, garlic salt, and white pepper in a third shallow bowl. Dredge the pork chops first in the flour, then the eggs, and finally the breadcrumb mixture and place on a baking sheet.

In a medium skillet over medium-high heat, heat about ¼ cup canola oil. Fry the pork chops one at a time until they are golden brown and cooked through, about 4 minutes per side. Transfer the chops to a plate lined with paper towel to absorb excess oil. Continue with the remaining chops, replenishing the oil as needed. Transfer to a wire rack placed over a baking sheet and keep warm in the oven at 200°F.

Serve the schnitzel with lemon wedges and parsley.

Diri Sos Pwa Legim

Paul Toussaint

SERVES 6 TO 8

PREP TIME: 1 hour + at least 1 hour and up to overnight marinating

COOK TIME: 2½ hours

EPIS

4 green onions, chopped

4 sprigs flat-leaf parsley

4 sprigs thyme

3 cloves garlic, peeled

1 Scotch bonnet pepper, seeded

½ green bell pepper, seeded and chopped

⅓ cup sour orange juice

¼ cup vegetable oil

2 tbsp complete seasoning

1 tbsp salt

LEGIM

900 g (2 lb) stewing meat (beef, pork shoulder, goat, or oxtail), cut into 1-inch cubes

2 limes, halved

1½ tsp salt, plus more to taste

⅓ cup epis (see above)

2 tsp vegetable oil

2 tbsp tomato paste

½ head cabbage, shredded

1 medium onion, thinly sliced

1 large eggplant, peeled and cut into ¼-inch dice

1 cup green beans, trimmed

1 chayote, peeled, pitted, and finely diced

1 green bell pepper, seeded and thinly sliced

1 carrot, peeled and thinly sliced

Continued

> 66 Diri sos pwa legim is a Haitian family meal that I grew up eating. My grandmother cooked it for me all the time—I even have a scar on my back from getting too close to the stove when it was being made for me! What's great about it is that it's hearty and healthy and has a mix of everything in it: the vegetables and meat provide a mix of vitamins and minerals, including iron. My son sees us eating this all the time, so it makes him want to eat it too. He knows it's my favourite meal, and now it's his favourite as well. Kids often won't eat their vegetables if they're raw—I know I didn't—but when they're cooked, they're softer and easier to eat. 99

MAKE THE EPIS: Place all the ingredients in a blender and blend until smooth. Store in an airtight jar in the fridge for up to 1 month or in the freezer for up to 6 months.

MAKE THE LEGIM: Place the meat in a medium bowl and squeeze the lime juice over it. Add the lime halves and sprinkle the meat with the salt. Using your hands, rub the salt and lime juice into the meat until all the pieces are thoroughly covered.

Rinse the meat with cold water and drain, discarding the lime halves. Add ⅓ cup of the epis to the meat and toss to coat. Let marinate in the fridge for 1 hour or up to overnight.

In a large pot, heat the oil over medium-low heat. Add the tomato paste and cook, stirring constantly, until the tomato paste starts caramelizing, about 1 to 2 minutes. Add the meat in a single layer and cover the pot, letting the meat sweat for 10 minutes. Do this in batches if necessary.

Turn the meat over, add all the vegetables (but not the Scotch bonnet pepper), and cover. Let simmer until the meat is very tender and the vegetables are soft, about 2 hours, stirring occasionally.

MEANWHILE, MAKE THE SOS PWA: In a medium pot, combine the beans, onion, garlic, water, and oil. Bring to a boil and reduce to a simmer. Cook for 1 hour, then add the coconut milk and cook for another 30 minutes, or until the beans are very tender. Add water as needed to keep the beans covered with liquid. Make a bouquet garni with the thyme and parsley.

Once the beans are tender, reserve ¼ cup of whole beans and place the rest in a food processor to purée into a smooth paste. Return the purée to the pot along with the reserved whole beans, bouquet garni, complete seasoning, Scotch bonnet, and salt and bring to a simmer.

Continued

1 bunch spinach

1 whole Scotch bonnet pepper

¼ cup sour orange juice

1 tbsp complete seasoning,
  or more to taste

SOS PWA

1 cup dried black beans,
  rinsed and drained

1 small yellow onion, halved

3 cloves garlic

5 cups water

3 tbsp olive oil

½ cup coconut milk

4 sprigs thyme

3 sprigs flat-leaf parsley

1 tbsp complete seasoning,
  or more to taste

1 whole Scotch bonnet pepper

2 tsp salt, plus more to taste

2 tbsp butter

DIRI BLAN

1 tbsp olive oil

1 green onion, finely chopped

1 clove garlic, minced

1 cup water

½ tsp salt

1 cup jasmine rice

1 tbsp butter

Cook until the mixture begins to thicken, about 15 minutes. Taste and adjust the seasoning. Carefully remove the Scotch bonnet and the bouquet garni and discard. Add the butter and mix until it is completely melted.

FINISH THE LEGIM: Remove the meat from the stew and set aside. Mash the vegetables with a potato masher or a wooden spoon. Return the meat to the pot and add the Scotch bonnet, sour orange juice, and complete seasoning. Turn the heat to medium and let the stew simmer for about 30 minutes, stirring often. Taste and adjust the seasoning as needed

MEANWHILE, MAKE THE DIRI BLAN: In a large pot over medium heat, heat the oil. Add the green onions and garlic and sauté for 5 minutes. Add the water and salt and bring to a boil. To remove starch from the rice, rinse the rice with cold water until the water runs clear, then add the rice to the boiling water.

When the liquid has almost completely evaporated, add the butter, reduce the heat to low, cover the pot for 15 to 20 minutes, then fluff with a fork.

TO SERVE: Serve the sos pwa and legim over the diri blan.

Easy Ribs

Kim Thúy

❝ There are only five ingredients in this recipe, and it takes only 5 minutes to prepare. The cooking is done by itself in the oven. It might seem too simple to satisfy your taste buds; however, it's got it all: salty, sweet, and sour. Of course, the secret is in the maple syrup, which gives elegance to the mix. My children love this recipe because it's when they're allowed to lick their fingers. ❞

SERVES 4 TO 6
PREP TIME: 5 minutes
COOK TIME: 2 hours + 10 minutes

1 tbsp vegetable oil

2 racks pork ribs

1 cup soy sauce

1 cup maple syrup

1 cup water

⅓ cup vinegar (any kind you like)

Preheat the oven to 375°F.

In a large Dutch oven over medium-high heat, heat the oil and brown the ribs on all sides. Remove the Dutch oven from the heat and set aside.

In a medium bowl, combine the remaining ingredients and then pour over the ribs. Bake until the ribs are golden and soft and the meat falls off the bone, about 2 hours.

Freya's Lamb Meat Bones

Raegan Steinberg

66 Lucky for us, our daughter Freya always loved her fruits and veggies, but when it came to eating chicken or meat, she needed a gentle nudge. However, one night, after devouring our favourite lamb dinner, we passed her a bone to gnaw on and she was thrilled, gripping the bone in both hands and nibbling off every little tender morsel of crispy fat and sweet and savoury meat. I think she may have been teething, but regardless, she loved to munch on that bone and has been doing so ever since. 99

SERVES 4

PREP TIME: 10 minutes +
1 hour 40 minutes resting

COOK TIME: 24 to 29 minutes

RIBS

900 g (2 lb) lamb ribs, loin removed (ask your butcher)

1 tbsp cumin seeds

2 tsp fennel seeds

1 tsp ground turmeric

2 tsp sugar

1 tsp salt

1 tbsp avocado oil

CUCUMBER SALAD

3 Lebanese cucumbers, sliced

Balsamic vinegar, to taste

Olive oil, to taste

Salt and pepper, to taste

MAKE THE RIBS: One hour before cooking, bring the ribs to room temperature. Preheat the oven to 325°F.

In a small skillet, toast the cumin and fennel seeds until fragrant. Let cool, then grind them into a powder using a spice grinder. Mix with the turmeric, sugar, and salt and set aside.

Coat the ribs with the avocado oil. Rub the spice mixture into the ribs, covering every inch. Let sit for 30 minutes.

Line a baking sheet with parchment paper and transfer the ribs to the sheet. Bake for 16 to 20 minutes, or until desired doneness. Freya likes hers medium. Turn the oven to broil and bake for another 3 to 4 minutes, watching the ribs carefully so they don't burn. Transfer to a plate, cover with aluminum foil and let rest for 10 minutes.

MEANWHILE, MAKE THE CUCUMBER SALAD: Toss the cucumbers with balsamic vinegar and olive oil, to taste. Season with salt and pepper.

TO SERVE: Cut the ribs into individual riblets and blow, blow, blow. Serve with the cucumber salad.

Herbed Lamb Meatballs in Tomato & Chickpea Stew

Renée Lavallée

SERVES 4

PREP TIME: 20 minutes

COOK TIME: 35 to 40 minutes

STEW

½ cup olive oil

2 medium onions, chopped

4 cloves garlic, minced

2 (796 ml/28 oz) cans San Marzano tomatoes, crushed

1 (540 ml/19 oz) can chickpeas, drained and rinsed

2 tsp ground cumin

2 tsp ground coriander

1 tsp ground allspice

1 tsp ground sumac

LAMB MEATBALLS

900 g (2 lb) coarsely ground lamb (or ground beef or pork)

1 tbsp chopped parsley

1 tbsp chopped fresh mint

1 tbsp chopped fresh oregano

1 tbsp chopped cilantro

2 tsp ground cumin

2 tsp ground coriander

1 tsp ground allspice

1 tsp crushed red pepper flakes (optional)

Salt and pepper, to taste

TO SERVE

2 tbsp finely chopped parsley

2 tbsp finely chopped cilantro

2 tbsp finely chopped fresh mint

4 eggs

❝ When I was a kid, my parents used to buy a whole lamb every year, and they would try to trick us into eating it by making "meatballs"; unfortunately, that didn't work. When I had my two kids, I remembered how my mom used to trick us into eating lamb, so I thought I would give it a shot. My kids love spice and spicy food, freshness, and things that are fun to eat. I came up with this recipe that satisfied both kids and kept Mom and Dad happy too! This hearty meal is great heated up the next day or put in the kids' thermoses for their lunches. They love it if there's naan or pita bread to sop up all the tasty tomato sauce too. I finish this dish with a few eggs that I simmer right in the sauce for added goodness. ❞

MAKE THE STEW: In a large pot over medium-high heat, heat the oil. Add the onions and cook until they are translucent and golden, about 5 minutes. Add the garlic and cook for a few minutes, stirring often to prevent scorching the garlic. Add the tomatoes, chickpeas, and spices, reduce the heat to a simmer, and let cook for about 25 minutes while you make the meatballs.

MAKE THE LAMB MEATBALLS: Preheat the oven to 425°F. Lightly oil a baking sheet and set aside.

In a large bowl, combine all the meatball ingredients and mix until the spices and herbs are well distributed. Shape the meat into golf-ball-sized meatballs and place them on the prepared baking sheet.

Bake until the meatballs are browned, about 15 to 20 minutes. Transfer the meatballs to the stew, scraping any browned bits stuck to the baking sheet and adding them as well. Taste and adjust the seasoning as needed. If storing for later use, pack in an airtight container in the fridge for up to 1 week, or the freezer for up to 3 months.

TO SERVE: Add the herbs to the stew and mix to combine. Crack the eggs on top of the sauce and cook, covered, until the eggs are cooked through, about 5 to 10 minutes. Serve over brown or basmati rice or with some naan or pita.

Meatball Sliders

Lora Kirk

SERVES 4 TO 6
PREP TIME: 30 minutes
COOK TIME: 52 to 55 minutes

MARINARA SAUCE

¼ cup olive oil

6 cloves garlic, thinly sliced

1 (796 ml/28 oz) can whole
    San Marzano tomatoes,
    crushed

1 cup water

1 tsp salt

1 tsp sugar

Pinch crushed red pepper flakes

2 large sprigs basil

MEATBALLS

225 g (½ lb) ground pork

225 g (½ lb) ground beef

½ cup panko breadcrumbs

¼ cup minced onion

2 tbsp chopped flat-leaf parsley

½ tbsp minced garlic

2 eggs, beaten

½ tsp salt

½ tsp pepper

TO SERVE

12 slider buns

Marinara sauce (see above)

2 cups shredded mozzarella

2 tbsp olive oil

GratedParmesan

> 66 My two little girls, Addie Pepper and Gemma Jet Aubergine, love this recipe, for it has all their favourites: cheese, tomato sauce, and soft buns! Also, this dish brings some fun to the dinner table, as the girls get to pull a cheesy slider off the casserole dish onto their plate, which means sometimes a very cheesy, stringy mess, again more fun for them. The other highlight is that sliders are just the right size for them, making them feel like they got a whole "burger" and not half or a quarter of a large one! 99

MAKE THE SAUCE: In a large skillet over medium heat, heat the oil. Add the garlic. As soon as it begins sizzling, add the tomatoes. Add the water to the tomato can and swirl to get all the juices, then add to the skillet. Add the salt, sugar, and red pepper flakes. Stir to combine.

Add the basil and simmer until the sauce is thickened and the oil on the surface is a deep orange, about 15 minutes. Remove the basil. Set aside. Store in the fridge for up to 1 week, or the freezer for up to 3 months.

MAKE THE MEATBALLS: Preheat the oven to 350°F. Line a baking sheet with parchment paper.

In a large bowl, combine the pork, beef, breadcrumbs, onions, parsley, garlic, eggs, salt, and pepper. Mix well. With lightly moistened hands, roll the mixture into 12 tablespoon-sized balls.

Place the meatballs on the prepared baking sheet and bake for 12 to 15 minutes. Remove from the oven.

TO SERVE: Place the bottom halves of the slider buns in a casserole dish. Spoon a little bit of the marinara sauce on each bun, then place a meatball on each one, topping with a bit more sauce. Cover the meatballs with mozzarella. Place the top halves of the buns on top of the meatballs. Brush them with a bit of oil and sprinkle with Parmesan.

Cover the casserole dish with aluminum foil and bake for 10 minutes, then uncover and continue baking for another 10 minutes. Serve with lots of napkins!

Healthy Hamburgers

Dan Geltner

66 Zucchini-beef burgers are the perfect way to add healthy veggies to your meal, while still serving delicious beefy burgers. Zucchinis are juicy when cooked and don't have a strong flavour, perfect for hiding in ground meat. **99**

SERVES 4
PREP TIME: 10 minutes
 + 10 to 15 minutes resting
COOK TIME: 20 minutes

2 medium zucchinis, grated

1 tsp salt

225 g (½ lb) ground beef

1 egg, beaten

Olive oil

4 hamburger buns, halved

Favourite burger garnishes
    to serve

In a medium bowl, combine the zucchini with half of the salt and let sit for 10 to 15 minutes. Squeeze out all the liquid from the zucchini and place them back in the bowl. Add the beef, the remaining salt, and the egg. Mix to combine. Shape into four patties.

In a medium skillet over medium heat, add a bit of oil. Toast the cut sides of the buns until they are golden. Set aside and cover to keep warm. Add a bit more olive oil and cook the burgers in batches for 3 to 5 minutes per side, until golden and cooked through.

Place the patties on the buns and top with your favourite toppings.

Frybread Tacos

Billy Alexander

" Tacos are always a popular choice in our house, and my daughter loves them because she can build her own however she likes. As with most meals we make, I try to build Indigenous ingredients or flavours into our daily lives, and these tacos are no exception. From the frybread to the bison, it's a fun and delicious way to enjoy tacos. **"**

SERVES 6 TO 8
PREP TIME: 25 minutes
COOK TIME: 45 minutes

FRYBREAD TACOS

3 cups all-purpose flour, plus more for dusting

1 tbsp baking powder

½ tsp salt

1½ cups warm water

3 cups vegetable oil

TACO FILLING

1 tbsp vegetable oil

900 g (2 lb) ground bison or beef

1 onion, diced

1 tbsp Cajun seasoning

Salt and pepper, to taste

TOPPINGS

250 g (9 oz) smoked Gouda, shredded

1½ cups diced tomatoes

1 head iceberg lettuce, shredded

2 cups sour cream

2 cups salsa

MAKE THE FRYBREAD TACOS: In a large bowl, combine the flour, baking powder, and salt and mix until combined. Make a small well in the middle of the flour mixture and add the warm water. Gently fold the flour mixture into the water, using a light touch, until the dough is completely homogeneous. Do not overmix the dough, as this will make it dense and heavy.

Place the dough on a lightly floured work surface and lightly knead it. Divide it into six to eight pieces, depending on the size you want. Roll each piece into a circle ¼-inch thick and use your thumb to make a small depression in the centre of each piece. This will prevent the dough from shrinking into a ball.

In a large cast-iron skillet, heat the oil until it reaches 350°F. Working in batches, carefully transfer the frybread to the oil and fry until each side is puffed up and golden, about 2 minutes per side. Transfer to paper towels to absorb excess oil, then transfer to a wire rack placed over a baking sheet and keep warm in the oven at 200°F. Continue frying the remaining breads.

MAKE THE FILLING: In a separate large skillet, heat the oil over medium heat. Add the bison or beef and onions and cook until the meat is browned and the onions are translucent, about 20 minutes. Add the Cajun seasoning and the salt and pepper to taste, and mix to combine.

TO SERVE: Place each frybread on a plate and top with the meat mixture, piled high. Add the smoked Gouda followed by the tomatoes and iceberg lettuce. Top with sour cream and salsa and serve with a knife and fork. Store any leftover tacos, separate from their fillings, in an airtight container at room temperature for up to 3 days.

Beef & Broccoli

Jonathan Cheung

66 Beef and broccoli is a weekly occurrence in my household. It's quick, flavourful, and so satisfying. Having that one back-pocket recipe that is 100% effective is invaluable, and this is mine. Dinnertime never goes as smoothly as it does when this dish is served. The key to getting that Chinese restaurant–like flare is to maintain a high temperature in your pan: a very hot temperature ensures crisp vegetables and juicy morsels of meat. 99

SERVES 4 TO 6
PREP TIME: 15 minutes
COOK TIME: about 10 minutes

2 heads broccoli

300 g (10 oz) tender beef
    (like top sirloin, strip loin,
    or tenderloin)

½ cup good-quality chicken stock

2 tbsp oyster sauce

2 tbsp Shaoxing rice wine

2 tsp superior dark soy sauce

1 tsp sesame oil

1 tbsp sugar

1 tbsp cornstarch

4 tbsp vegetable oil

2 cloves garlic, finely minced

1 tsp grated fresh ginger

Cooked jasmine rice, to serve

Cut the broccoli florets into bite-sized pieces, trim the stock, and slice thinly; set aside. Slice the beef into very thin slices and set aside.

For the sauce, whisk together the stock, oyster sauce, rice wine, soy sauce, sesame oil, sugar, and cornstarch.

Heat a wok or frying pan over high heat. When very hot, add 2 tablespoons of the vegetable oil and the sliced beef. Do not stir for the first 30 seconds. After 30 seconds, stir quickly and allow to cook for 1 to 2 minutes, or until the beef is mostly cooked through. Remove from the pan and set aside.

Wash the pan and return to high heat. When hot, add the remaining 2 tablespoons of oil. Toss in the broccoli and stir-fry for 2 to 3 minutes. Add the garlic and ginger and toss to combine. Return the meat to the pan, along with the sauce. Stir to combine. Bring to a simmer and allow to simmer for 3 to 4 minutes. Serve with cooked jasmine rice.

Filet Mignon & Frites

Fred Morin

66 Go to the butcher and buy some nice filet mignon. It's a gateway meat for kids going from ground beef to a way nicer cut, but still mild in flavour and tender—like the Twist Shandy of meat. And when your kids grow up and have to cook something fancy to impress a partner or potential partner, if they know how to cook filet mignon, they're going to be a catch. You'll need sharp knives for this one, and the kids can help by introducing a rational but substantiated fear of blades. Get out Grandma's old silver carving set and trust them with the horn-handled plated silver Birks family heirloom—they'll surprise you (hopefully) with their knife skills. **99**

SERVES 4

PREP TIME: 20 minutes

COOK TIME: 30 minutes

2 filets mignons
    (about 175 g/6 oz each)

Salt and pepper, to taste

2 tsp vegetable oil

1 knob butter

1 splash cognac

1 cup beef broth

1 cup heavy cream, lightly whisked

4 cups vegetable oil, for frying

454 g (1 lb) Yukon Gold potatoes,
    peeled and cut into fries

Remove the meat from the fridge 1 hour before cooking, unless you live in a jungle climate or have a lot of cats (nothing against cats). Salt and pepper the meat.

In a medium skillet over medium-high heat, add the oil and butter and sear the meat, about 2 minutes on each side for a steak the size of a pack of cards. Remove the pan from the heat and sprinkle the steak with a good pinch of pepper. Let the meat rest on a cutting board.

Put the pan back on the heat and deglaze with a splash of cognac (this is where you can show off and flambé it). Add the broth and let it reduce by half. Whisk in the cream. (You can eventually sneak in incrementally complex, smelly items like blue cheese or Dijon mustard, or even a few snails.)

In a deep fryer or large heavy-bottomed pot, heat the oil to 290°F. Add the potatoes in batches, if necessary, and fry until softened. Remove the potatoes from the oil and let drain on a baking sheet. Heat the oil to 340°F. Fry the potatoes in batches again, this time frying until golden brown. Remove from the oil and season with salt. Serve immediately.

Grilled Beef Striploin Steak

Joe Thottungal

66 Teaching my kids to cook has been delightful—and vital, in my opinion, for their adult lives. I find the most enjoyable time to be when we are tasting and making adjustments to the food as we go along. This recipe is very easy to make and comforting to the soul—when we have come back from a trip or even just a long day out, a grilled steak with Deccan Dal & Spinach (page 43) is just the thing to welcome us back home. I believe food has power and that we can express our love through it—if ever you need to impress someone, just put all your feelings into your cooking and that person will be blown away. **99**

SERVES 4 TO 6

PREP TIME: 2 minutes + 3 hours marinating + 1 hour resting

COOK TIME: 12 minutes + 10 minutes resting

STEAKS

3 striploin steaks, cut 1 inch thick (about 1 kg/2.2 lb)

1 tbsp + ½ tsp garam masala (see below)

1 tbsp salt

1 tbsp pepper

½ tbsp crushed red pepper flakes

8 cloves garlic, minced

1 sprig rosemary, chopped

1 sprig thyme, chopped

2 tbsp olive oil

2 tbsp whole-grain mustard

GARAM MASALA

1 tbsp fennel seeds

1 tsp cardamom pods

1 tsp whole cloves

1 star anise

1 cinnamon stick (½-inch long)

Deccan Dal & Spinach (page 43), to serve

PREPARE THE STEAKS: Using a paper towel, pat the steaks dry and set them aside.

MAKE THE GARAM MASALA: In a dry frying pan over medium heat, toast the spices until fragrant, stirring constantly, about 2 minutes. Transfer to a spice mill or mortar and pestle and grind to a fine powder.

MAKE THE STEAKS: In a small bowl, combine 1 tablespoon of the garam masala, the salt, pepper, red pepper flakes, garlic, herbs, oil, and mustard. Rub the spiced oil on the steaks, cover, and refrigerate for at least 3 hours.

Bring the steaks to room temperature 1 hour before grilling.

Heat the grill to 350°F. Place the steaks on the grill and cook for 3 minutes. Rotate the steaks 90 degrees and cook for another 3 minutes to get good grill marks. Flip the steaks and cook for another 3 minutes before turning 90 degrees once again and cooking to the desired doneness.

TO SERVE: Remove the steaks from the grill and sprinkle the remaining garam masala over them. Let them rest for at least 10 minutes. Slice the steaks across the grain and serve over the Deccan Dal & Spinach (page 43). Enjoy.

NOTE: I suggest that you never purchase garam masala. Rather, make your own in small batches when you need it. It can be stored in an airtight container for up to 6 months.

Moose Stew

Jeremy Charles

66 Whether it's to eat on a cold winter evening by the fire or as a shore lunch while fly-fishing for salmon, my son, Hank, loves a bowl of moose stew. It's wild and organic, and he finds the stories behind the hunt captivating. It's a true staple for our family. 99

SERVES 6 TO 8
PREP TIME: 20 minutes
COOK TIME: 2 hours 20 minutes

900 g (2 lb) cubed moose meat
   (shoulder or neck)

2 tbsp all-purpose flour

3 tbsp vegetable oil

3 medium yellow onions, diced

3 large Yukon Gold potatoes,
   peeled and diced

3 large carrots, diced

1 medium rutabaga, diced

3 cloves garlic, minced

2 tbsp tomato paste

1 small bunch thyme

2 fresh bay leaves

6 cups moose stock
   (or chicken or vegetable)

Salt and pepper, to taste

Preheat the oven to 300°F.

In a medium bowl, toss the moose meat with the flour until evenly coated. In a large oven-safe pot over medium heat, heat the oil. Add the moose meat and cook until brown on all sides, about 5 minutes.

Add the onions, potatoes, carrots, rutabaga, garlic, tomato paste, thyme, and bay leaves and cook over medium-low heat for about 7 minutes. Add the stock, bring to a boil, then reduce the heat and simmer for about 8 minutes.

Cover the pot and place in the oven. Bake for 2 hours, or until the meat is tender. Season to taste with salt and pepper and serve. Store in an airtight container in the freezer for up to 3 months.

Desserts & Drinks

Well, you've made it this far, which means you can finally give your kids the dessert that you've been using as bribery for them to finish their meal. But really, when you were young, was there anything better in life than dessert? I don't think so. Oh, and there are a few fun drinks in here for good measure.

Pumpkin Bran Muffins

Christa Bruneau-Guenther

66 What kid doesn't love a "cupcake" with icing? I have three children of my own (now adults), and before owning a restaurant, I owned and ran a licensed daycare. Being a health-conscious mother and caregiver, I always looked for ways to make healthy dessert alternatives—and this muffin "cupcake" was an all-time favourite among all the kids. The secret is the icing—when you add food colouring and a few sprinkles, kids will devour the whole thing!

It has always been very important to me to incorporate Indigenous ancestral ingredients into our diet. We are caregivers of the land, and I grow many ancestral ingredients in my garden. Growing, harvesting, and cooking them together with my children has been time well spent—like we did for the pumpkin in this recipe. I found baking was often the easiest way to coax the kids to cook with me in the kitchen—another reason this recipe is a favourite of mine—and I look forward to doing so with my grandchildren one day too! **99**

MAKES 12 MUFFINS
PREP TIME: 20 minutes
COOK TIME: 20 to 25 minutes

MUFFINS

¾ cup wheat bran flakes

¾ cup whole wheat flour

½ cup packed brown sugar

¼ cup sugar

1½ tsp ground cinnamon

1 tsp baking powder

1 tsp baking soda

1 tsp salt

1 cup canned or freshly cooked
   pumpkin purée

1 egg + 1 egg yolk

½ cup plain yogurt

⅓ cup grapeseed, canola, or
   vegetable oil

¼ cup raisins or chopped walnuts
   (or a combination)

ICING

½ cup cream cheese, at room
   temperature

3 tbsp icing sugar

2 drops food colouring (optional)

Rainbow sprinkles (optional)

MAKE THE MUFFINS: Preheat the oven to 400°F. Line a 12-cup muffin tin with paper liners, or lightly grease the tin. Set aside.

In a large bowl, combine the bran, flour, both sugars, cinnamon, baking powder, baking soda, and salt. Stir to combine.

In a medium bowl, whisk together the pumpkin purée, egg and egg yolk, yogurt, and oil. Add this to the large bowl of dry ingredients and mix to just combine. Do not overmix. Transfer the batter to the muffin tin.

Bake for 20 to 25 minutes, or until the muffins are golden brown and spring back to the touch. Remove from the oven and let cool on a cooling rack before icing.

MAKE THE ICING: In a small bowl, combine the cream cheese and icing sugar until smooth and creamy. Add food colouring, if desired.

Once the muffins are cool, top them with the icing and sprinkles. Store in an airtight container in the fridge for up to 5 days or freezer for up to 3 months.

Olibollen

Andrea Callan

66 When I was growing up, my family would make this recipe every year for New Year's Eve. In the evening after our dinner, we would start making it just in time to see the ball drop. Olibollen translates to "oil balls," but they are far from that—these are delicious, hot, fluffy doughnuts, served with side bowls of icing sugar. For us kids, there were no rules about how much icing sugar we used; it was more about the celebration of a new year. I have golden memories of our family working together to make these, newspaper under the deep fryer in our garage, and big sugary smiles. 99

MAKES 24 DOUGHNUTS
PREP TIME: 30 minutes + 1½ hours rising
COOK TIME: 15 to 25 minutes

2 cups lukewarm milk

2 tbsp sugar

1 tbsp instant yeast

2 eggs

½ tsp vanilla

½ tsp salt

4 cups all-purpose flour

¼ tsp ground cinnamon

¼ tsp ground nutmeg

3 medium apples, peeled, cored, and diced

2 cups golden raisins

Canola oil, for frying

Icing sugar, for tossing

In a large bowl, combine ½ cup of the lukewarm milk with the sugar and yeast, and stir. Let sit for 10 minutes. Add the remaining milk, the eggs, vanilla, and salt and stir until well mixed.

In another large bowl, combine the flour, cinnamon, and nutmeg. Add the apples and raisins and toss to coat them in the flour mixture. Add the dry fruit mixture to the bowl with the batter and mix gently to combine. Cover and let rise at room temperature for 1½ hours.

Preheat your deep fryer, or heat your oil (about 3 inches deep) in a deep skillet, to 375°F. Working in batches, drop ¼ cup of batter per doughnut into the oil, and fry until golden brown, about 1 to 2 minutes per side. Transfer to a paper-towel-lined baking sheet to remove excess oil. Repeat with the rest of the batter. Serve warm with bowls of icing sugar to dip the doughnuts in. Store in an airtight container at room temperature for up to 3 days.

King Kong Junior Cookies

Dyan Solomon

" Olive + Gourmando is kid heaven, mostly because of the crazy-packed dessert and pastry table we have right up front. When kids come in, I watch their eyes zero in on the sweets immediately—it's pretty amazing. Now, you would think that it's the chocolaty stuff that would be the biggest draw for our youngest customers, but surprisingly, it's our King Kong cookies with banana purée in the batter (what kid doesn't like bananas?). I've been slightly sneaky here and adapted the Olive recipe to make it healthier without sacrificing taste—hence the Junior—so you won't feel so bad if the kiddos want seconds. Add ½ cup chocolate chips for a treat, and depending on allergies, feel free to toss in ½ cup of any kind of nut. Otherwise, this version is yummy as is. "

MAKES 15 LARGE COOKIES
PREP TIME: 30 minutes
COOK TIME: 12 minutes per batch

¾ cup + ½ tsp all-purpose flour

½ cup whole wheat flour

½ tsp baking soda

1 tsp salt

¾ cup butter, at room
  temperature

½ cup sugar

½ cup packed brown sugar

1 egg, at room temperature

2 tsp vanilla

2 medium ripe bananas, mashed

1 cup old-fashioned oats

Preheat the oven to 375°F. Line two or three baking sheets with parchment paper or silicone mats. Set aside.

In a bowl, combine the flours, baking soda, and salt and set aside.

In a stand mixer fitted with the paddle attachment, or with a hand mixer, cream the butter and sugars on medium speed for 3 minutes, or until the mixture is pale and creamy. Add the egg and vanilla and mix on high for 2 minutes, until the texture is uniform, then add the bananas and continue mixing for 1 minute. Add the flour mixture and mix on low until just combined. Remove the bowl from the mixer and add the oats. Using a wooden spoon, gently mix.

Using an ice-cream scoop or soup spoon, scoop the batter into balls and place on the baking sheets, leaving 3 inches between each cookie. Flatten the cookies with the palm of your hand until they are ⅓-inch thick.

Bake for 12 minutes, one sheet at a time, rotating the sheet halfway through. Place the sheets on cooling racks and let the cookies cool on the sheets. Then go bananas! Store in an airtight container at room temperature for up to 1 week, or the freezer for up to 1 month.

Chocolate Chip Cookies

Katie & Shane Hayes

❝ This is our go-to dessert: it's the recipe we use to make cookies at our restaurant, and kids always flock to them. My kids want to make them for every school or birthday gathering. They are "gooey and oozy," as the kids would say. The batter should sit overnight in the fridge, if possible; this stops the cookies from spreading while baking. **❞**

MAKES ABOUT 40 COOKIES

PREP TIME: 20 minutes + 4 hours to overnight resting

COOK TIME: 8 to 12 minutes per batch

1⅓ cups butter, softened

1¼ cups sugar

1¼ cups lightly packed brown sugar

2 tsp salt

4 eggs

2 tsp vanilla

4 cups all-purpose flour

2 tsp baking soda

4 cups dark chocolate chips

In a stand mixer fitted with the paddle attachment, or using an electric mixer, cream together the butter, sugars, and salt. Slowly add the eggs, one at a time, beating well after each addition, followed by the vanilla. Remove the bowl from the mixer and gently fold in the flour and baking soda, followed by the chocolate chips.

Cover the bowl with plastic wrap and place in the fridge for 4 hours, or ideally overnight.

Preheat the oven to 375°F. Line a baking sheet with parchment paper.

Using an ice-cream scoop or a large spoon, drop balls of dough onto the baking sheet, leaving 2 inches between each cookie.

Bake for 8 to 12 minutes. The cookies will look soft, but they will harden as they cool. Place the baking sheet on a cooling rack and let cool.

If you don't want to bake up all the cookies, the remaining dough can be portioned, placed on a parchment-paper-lined tray, and frozen. Store the frozen dough balls in a sealable plastic bag in the freezer for up to 1 month. Bake directly from frozen, adding another 2 to 3 minutes to the baking time.

Chocolate Chocolate Chip Cookies (aka Santa Cookies)

Joanna Fox

66 My mom used to make my son chocolate chip cookies, which he was totally obsessed with, but this one time, right before Christmas, she decided to switch it up and made him chocolate chocolate chip cookies instead. BIG mistake. He didn't even want to look at them. So when it was time to leave out cookies and milk for Santa on Christmas Eve, guess which cookies Santa was given? Well, when we woke up and my son saw that Santa had devoured the cookies he didn't like, his interest was piqued. If Santa liked them. . . They're now a staple in our house, and my son's go-to dessert, regardless of the season. **99**

MAKES ABOUT 36 COOKIES
PREP TIME: 15 minutes + 2 hours chilling
COOK TIME: 8 to 10 minutes per batch

1⅓ cups butter, at
    room temperature

1 cup sugar

⅔ cup lightly packed brown sugar

2 eggs

1 tsp vanilla

2¼ cups all-purpose flour

⅔ cup cocoa powder

1 tsp baking soda

¼ cup milk

2 cups chocolate chips
    (or 1 cup chocolate chips,
    + 1 cup chopped pecans)

Photo on page 251

In a stand mixer fitted with the paddle attachment, or using an electric mixer, cream together the butter and sugars until fluffy. Beat in the eggs and vanilla.

In a small bowl, sift together the flour, cocoa powder, and baking soda. Add to the butter mixture, a third at a time, alternating with the milk. Stir in the chocolate chips (and nuts, if using). Place the cookie batter in the fridge and chill for 2 hours until firm.

Preheat the oven to 350°F. Line a baking sheet with parchment paper. Place 12 tablespoon-sized mounds of batter onto the baking sheet 2 inches apart. Bake for 8 to 10 minutes, or until crisp. Repeat two more times, with another 12 cookies in each batch. Store in an airtight container at room temperature for up to 1 week, or in the freezer for 2 months.

Brownies with Cream Cheese Frosting & Rainbow Sprinkles

Lora Kirk

❝ My girls' favourite recipe, hands down, is for these brownies with cream cheese frosting and rainbow sprinkles. I mean, c'mon, what's not to love? **❞**

MAKES 12 BROWNIES
PREP TIME: 15 minutes
COOK TIME: 30 minutes

BROWNIES

340 g (12 oz) dark chocolate, chopped

1¼ cups butter, plus more for pan

1¼ cups all-purpose flour, plus more for pan

⅓ cup cocoa powder

½ tsp salt

2½ cups sugar

5 eggs

1½ tbsp vanilla

1 cup milk chocolate chips

ICING

½ cup cream cheese

2 tbsp butter

2 cups icing sugar

¼ cup rainbow sprinkles

Preheat the oven to 350°F. Butter and flour a 9 × 13-inch baking pan. Set aside.

MAKE THE BROWNIES: In a medium heatproof bowl, add the chocolate and butter. Place the bowl over a small pot of simmering water and stir occasionally until the chocolate is melted. Remove from the heat and let cool.

In a medium bowl, whisk together the flour, cocoa, and salt, until well mixed. Set aside.

Once the chocolate mixture has cooled, add to it the sugar, eggs, and vanilla and mix until combined. Fold the flour mixture into the chocolate mixture, followed by the chocolate chips.

Transfer the batter to the prepared baking pan. Bake until a toothpick inserted into the middle of the pan comes out clean, about 25 minutes. Remove from the oven and let cool.

MAKE THE ICING: Combine the cream cheese and butter in the bowl of a stand mixer fitted with the whisk attachment (or use an electric mixer) and beat until creamy and smooth. With the mixer on low, gradually add the icing sugar until completely combined.

Once the brownies are cool, frost the top with the icing and decorate with rainbow sprinkles. Store in an airtight container in the fridge for up to 1 week, or the freezer for up to 1 month.

Gourmet Goo Skillet Brownies

Anna Olson

> ❝ I started play-baking before I was old enough to understand what a recipe was. When I asked to help in the kitchen, my mom would pull out random ingredients that usually included day-old bread, eggs, sugar, milk, and chocolate chips. I could mix them any way I chose, and Mom would bake the concoction up as I parked myself in front of the oven to watch. Naturally, Mom would pronounce the dish delicious upon the first bite (was there ever a second?), naming it "Gourmet Goo." That gesture of love and patience has inspired this mess of a warm brownie, which is perfect for learning how to mix, stir, crack eggs, and more, and is forgiving if the measurements aren't precise. The magic really happens in the oven as the ingredients bake up into a gooey, sweet wonder. ❞

SERVES 8 TO 12
PREP TIME: 10 minutes
COOK TIME: 30 to 35 minutes

½ cup butter

½ cup (115 g/4 oz) dark couverture/ baking chocolate, chopped

1 cup sugar

2 eggs, at room temperature

1 tsp vanilla

⅓ cup all-purpose flour

¼ cup cocoa powder

½ tsp fine salt

¼ tsp baking powder

1½ cups coarsely chopped treats (cookies, candies, chocolate bars, chocolate chips)

10 to 12 large marshmallows, halved

Chocolate fudge sauce and/or butterscotch sauce, warmed, to serve

Vanilla ice cream, to serve

Preheat the oven to 350°F. Butter a 9-inch skillet or cake pan. Set aside.

In a small saucepan over low heat, melt the butter and baking chocolate, stirring constantly until they are melted and smooth. You can do this step in the microwave, stirring every 10 seconds. Transfer the mixture to a large bowl. Add the sugar and whisk to combine. Add the eggs one at a time, mixing well before each addition. Add the vanilla.

Sift the dry ingredients together and add them to the chocolate mixture all at once, stirring until well combined. Fold in 1 cup of the treats and transfer the batter to the prepared skillet, evening out the top.

Bake for 20 to 25 minutes, until the sides begin to come away from the pan and the top of the brownie begins to lose its shine. Remove the brownie from the oven and raise the oven temperature to 400°F. Arrange the marshmallows and the remaining treats on top of the brownie and bake for another 5 minutes to brown the marshmallows.

Let cool on a cooling rack for 15 minutes before drizzling with warm fudge and/or butterscotch sauce. Serve warm topped with ice cream.

If you are not serving the brownie right away, do not top with sauce. Let cool, cut into squares, and store in an airtight container at room temperature for up to 3 days.

Coconut Cream Bars

Raquel Fox

"" As a child, I craved these coconut bars more than candy. They are a sentimental treat from my childhood, my grandmother's reward system for acts of kindness, maintaining good grades, or simply "just because." My aunt Tia perfected this chewy, creamy treat, which is made without cream, and I made it healthier by replacing red food colouring with beet juice. These bars were highly requested during school events, so naturally the tradition continued with my kids. One bite was always followed by a kid saying, "I wish my mom made these!" And then it happened. . . the most prideful smile on my son's face. ""

MAKES 16 SQUARES
PREP TIME: 5 minutes + 8 hours setting
COOK TIME: 20 to 30 minutes

2 cups frozen grated coconut, thawed

2 cups sugar

¼ tsp salt

½ cup water

3 tbsp beet juice or purée

In a medium saucepan, combine the coconut, sugar, salt, and water. Cook over medium heat, stirring occasionally, until the water evaporates, about 20 to 30 minutes. Pack half the coconut mixture into the bottom of an 8-inch square baking pan, smoothing out the top with an offset spatula.

Using an electric mixer, beat the remaining coconut mixture until it becomes fluffy, about 30 seconds. Add the beet juice and stir until the mixture is homogeneous. Transfer to the baking pan and press lightly to adhere the two layers. Smooth out the top.

Cover the pan with a cloth or paper towel and let set for 8 hours at room temperature. Cut into sixteen 2-inch squares. Set on a plate and watch as they quickly disappear. Store in an airtight container in the fridge for up to 1 week, or the freezer for up to 1 month.

Confetti Angel Food Cake

Camilla Wynne

❝ Confetti angel food cake from a boxed mix was hands down my favourite childhood cake, but the homemade version is superior, especially when cloaked in swathes of buttermilk whipped cream. Just don't go easy on the sprinkles. **❞**

MAKES ONE 10-INCH CAKE
PREP TIME: 20 minutes
COOK TIME: 40 to 45 minutes

CAKE

1 cup cake flour

1½ cups sugar

11 egg whites,
   at room temperature

2 tbsp lemon juice

1 tsp vanilla paste

¼ tsp salt

¼ cup rainbow sprinkles

ICING

1 cup heavy cream

¼ cup buttermilk

¼ cup icing sugar

1 tsp vanilla extract

Rainbow sprinkles

Preheat the oven to 350°F. Have a 10-inch tube pan at the ready, but do not butter or grease it. This cake needs to climb up the sides of the pan to achieve its lofty heights.

MAKE THE CAKE: In a bowl, sift the cake flour with ½ cup of the sugar.

In a stand mixer fitted with the whisk attachment, beat the egg whites on medium speed until white and foamy. Add the lemon juice, vanilla paste, and salt and increase the speed to medium-high. Beat until soft peaks form, then gradually add the remaining 1 cup of sugar. Continue to beat until stiff peaks form (where the tip of the peak just falls over). Remove the whisk and take the mixer bowl off the stand.

Sprinkle a third of the sifted flour and sugar mixture over the whites and, using your clean bare hand, fold it in. Your hand is your best tool here, as you can feel any pockets of unmixed flour and gently disperse them. Repeat twice more. Add the sprinkles and fold them in gently with a spatula just until evenly incorporated.

Transfer the batter to the pan, smoothing out the top.

Bake for 40 to 45 minutes, until golden and firm and a toothpick inserted in the cake comes out clean. Immediately invert and let cool completely. If your pan has little legs for inversion, that's perfect. Otherwise, put the hole over the neck of a wine bottle.

Once cool, use a metal spatula to loosen the cake from the pan before unmoulding onto a serving plate.

MAKE THE ICING: In a stand mixer fitted with the whisk attachment, whip the cream, buttermilk, icing sugar, and vanilla on medium-high speed until stiff peaks form.

With the help of a palette knife or mini offset spatula, frost the cake with the whipped cream. Decorate generously with sprinkles.

This cake is best the day it is made, but leftovers can be stored in an airtight container in the fridge for up to 2 days.

Sugar-Free, Gluten-Free Wild Blueberry Lemon Cucuzza Cake

Rob Gentile

❝ Cucuzza is Sicilian zucchini, and this cake was created by our family because we are fascinated with growing it in our garden (but you can use any type of zucchini in the cake). This recipe is great for kids, and my daughter, Clarice, loves to be involved in the process. When we prep, I measure out all the ingredients and her job is to add them, one by one, into the mixing bowl. This recipe is super healthy because it's sugar- and gluten-free. To sweeten it we use monk fruit powder—a natural sweetener that's non-glycemic—and instead of traditional flour we use oat flour and ground almonds. This cake is just as delicious as any blueberry lemon cake out there, and my sugar-obsessed daughter doesn't know the difference, so that's a huge win for any parent! ❞

MAKES 1 CAKE

PREP TIME: 25 minutes

COOK TIME: 1 to 1½ hours

CAKE

¾ cup butter,
   at room temperature

1 cup monk fruit powder

3 eggs, at room temperature

1¼ tsp vanilla

1 tbsp lemon juice

1 tbsp lemon zest

1½ cups oat flour

3 tsp baking powder

2 tsp xanthan gum

1½ cups ground almonds

½ tsp sea salt

1½ cups grated and squeezed dry
   cucuzza (Sicilian) or regular
   zucchini

1½ cups fresh or frozen wild
   blueberries

ICING

½ cup monk fruit powder

8 tsp lemon juice

MAKE THE CAKE: Preheat the oven to 350°F. Butter a loaf pan and line with parchment paper. Set aside.

In a stand mixer fitted with the paddle attachment, combine the butter and monk fruit powder and mix on high speed until light and fluffy, about 5 to 7 minutes. Scrape down the sides of the bowl with a spatula.

Add the eggs one by one, mixing until fully incorporated and emulsified between additions. Add the vanilla, lemon juice and lemon zest and mix until emulsified. This procedure can take up to 15 minutes. If your ingredients are not at room temperature, you can use a kitchen blowtorch to gently warm the mixing bowl and encourage emulsification.

In a medium bowl, sift the oat flour, baking powder, and xanthan gum together. Add the ground almonds and sea salt. With the mixer on low, gently add these dry ingredients to the butter mixture and mix until incorporated. Scrape the sides of the bowl with a spatula.

With the mixer on low, add the zucchini and mix until just incorporated. Lastly, fold in the blueberries.

Transfer the batter to the prepared loaf pan, smoothing it out with a spatula. The batter will be unusually dry because it is gluten-free. That's okay.

Bake for 1 hour if using fresh blueberries or 1½ hours if using frozen, or until the cake is golden brown and a toothpick inserted into the centre comes out clean. Allow the cake to cool completely before removing from the pan.

MAKE THE ICING: Combine the monk fruit powder and lemon juice in a small bowl and whisk until the monk fruit has dissolved. Drizzle over the cool cake and let set for 30 minutes. Slice thickly and enjoy! Store in an airtight container at room temperature for up to 3 days, or in the freezer for 1 month.

Apple, Pear, Caramel Pie

Stéphanie Labelle

❝ A lot of baking was happening in the house when I was growing up, just like many other chefs I would guess. Pancakes (even for dinner), summer fruit puddings, orange birthday cake, holiday cookies (a lot of them), pavlova. . . but never pies. My mom just didn't get around to it, and for some reason was never able to master a proper dough. I enjoyed plenty of pies baked by my aunt and grandma, but I was always too sacred to make my own—a fear I inherited from my mom I wonder? I got to culinary school without ever having made the simplest apple pie. . . which is what we did on the very first day! So here is the version I now make my nieces and nephew, and I always score points with the caramel twist. ❞

MAKES ONE 9-INCH PIE

PREP TIME: 30 minutes + 30 minutes chilling

COOK TIME: 1 hour 15 minutes

CRUST

2½ cups all-purpose flour

1 cup butter, very cold

½ tsp salt

½ cup ice-cold water

FILLING

4 apples, peeled, cored, and cut into ¼-inch slices

4 pears, peeled, cored, and cut into ¼-inch slices

¾ cup sugar

2 tbsp cornstarch

1 tsp ground cardamom

½ vanilla bean, halved and seeds scraped into the sugar

CARAMEL

1 cup heavy cream

1¼ cups sugar

1 tbsp butter

1 tsp fleur de sel

Continued

MAKE THE CRUST: In the bowl of a food processor, combine the flour, butter, and salt and pulse until the butter is pea-sized. Transfer the flour mixture to a clean work surface. Make a well in the centre of the flour and add the water. Working your way out from the centre in concentric circles, gradually mix the flour into the water until the dough comes together. Do not overmix.

Shape the dough into a disc and wrap in plastic wrap. Place in the fridge for 30 minutes to relax the dough.

MAKE THE FILLING: In a large bowl, toss the apple and pear slices with the sugar, cornstarch, ground cardamon, and vanilla bean until well mixed.

MAKE THE CARAMEL: This should have your full attention: no answering the phone or any other distractions. Keep your eyes on the pot!

In a small pot, bring the cream to a boil and set aside.

In small heavy-bottomed pot, heat ¼ cup of the sugar over medium heat. When the sugar has dissolved, add ¼ cup more sugar and gently stir using a heatproof spatula. Continue until all the sugar has been added.

Cook until the sugar turns a light brown colour, then quickly add the hot cream. Careful, as it can splatter. Heat the caramel until it reaches 235°F on a candy thermometer, then remove from the heat. Add the butter and salt, stir to combine, and set aside.

Continued

TO FINISH

1 egg

Pinch salt

Raw sugar, for sprinkling

FINISH THE PIE: Preheat the oven to 400°F.

Remove the dough from the fridge and warm it up using your hands. Transfer the dough to a lightly floured work surface and cut in half.

Lightly dust one half of the dough with flour and roll it out to a circle about 11 inches in diameter. Transfer the dough in a 9-inch pie plate. Add half of the caramel in one layer, followed by the apple-pear mixture. Brush the edge of the dough with a bit of water.

Roll out the remaining dough to a circle about 10 inches in diameter. Transfer to the top of the pie and carefully pinch the edges of the doughs together to seal the crust. Crimp the edge with a fork and cut off the excess dough with a sharp knife.

In a small bowl, beat the egg with a pinch of salt. Brush the top crust with this egg wash and sprinkle with raw sugar. Using a sharp knife, cut a few vents in the top crust.

Bake until the pie starts to turn golden, about 30 minutes. Lower the temperature to 350°F and bake until the crust is amber, about 30 minutes more. Place on a cooling rack and let cool. Serve with the remaining caramel sauce and some ice cream. Store in the fridge for up to 1 week, or the freezer for up to 3 months.

Flaming Banana Split with Hot Chocolate Sauce

Michael Smith

❝ Every family needs a showstopper now and then, and this one's for all the dads who never get near the kitchen. If you want to show your kids you can be a kitchen hero too, this is the dish for you. Swing for the fence with that flambé and cook up some memories while you're at it! **❞**

SERVES 4
PREP TIME: 15 minutes + 1 hour chilling
COOK TIME: 10 minutes

SAUCE

2 cups heavy cream

½ cup lightly packed brown sugar

1 tbsp cocoa powder

¼ tsp allspice

1 tbsp vanilla

1 tsp favourite hot sauce

225 g (8 oz) dark chocolate,
 broken into small pieces

BANANAS

¼ cup butter

½ cup lightly packed brown sugar

4 ripe bananas

¼ cup spiced rum

TO SERVE

Vanilla ice cream

Whipped cream

Sprinkles

MAKE THE SAUCE: In a medium saucepan, combine the cream, sugar, cocoa, allspice, vanilla, and hot sauce. Cook over medium-high heat, whisking constantly, until it comes to a simmer. Take the sauce off the heat and add the chocolate pieces, whisking until the sauce is smooth and the chocolate fully melted. Pour the sauce into a jar and refrigerate until thick, about 1 hour.

FLAMBÉ THE BANANAS: If you haven't flambéed before, practise beforehand. Use a small amount of rum and a knob of butter, without the sugar and bananas, and follow the instructions below for flambéeing so you know what to expect when you do it for real.

Preheat your largest, heaviest skillet or sauté pan over medium-high heat. Add the butter and swirl the pan gently until it sizzles and is fully melted. Add the sugar and continue swirling until the sugar is melted. Add the bananas and swirl, stir, and flip until the bananas are evenly coated and sizzling merrily, about 3 to 4 minutes.

For a gas stove: Extend your arm, swirling the sizzling pan away from the flame, and tilt the far edge of the pan down and away from you. Pour the rum into the bottom corner with the bananas. Keeping your arm safely extended, swing the pan back into the flame until the contents ignite.

For an electric stove: Pour the rum into the bananas as above. Ignite by holding the edge of the sizzling pan near a candle or barbecue lighter.

Hold steadily as the flame and applause erupt. Sauté as the flames die down, just a few moments longer, swirling the pan sauce together.

TO SERVE: Enthusiastically and extravagantly build banana splits with some ice cream, the bananas and hot chocolate sauce, and your choice of embellishments, like whipped cream and sprinkles!

Baked Strawberry Sherbet

Celeste Mah

❝ When summer finally comes to Newfoundland, you can definitely feel it, and I don't just mean temperature-wise. Our summer may be short, but everyone fully embraces it, and no one takes it for granted. One sure sign that summer has arrived is fresh strawberries. We're a bit behind the rest of the country when strawberries are finally in season here—they usually don't start popping up until about the middle of June. This recipe came to be when my husband and stepson went to the U-pick at Lester's Farm Market and gathered a lot of berries. We ate as many as we could, but by the time we got to the last of them, they were too soft to eat. They were still good enough to cook with, though, so I sprinkled some sugar on them, threw them in the oven, and made a baked strawberry sherbet. By baking the strawberries, you get this great jammy flavour, and if you want a little taste of summer in the winter, you can make it with frozen berries! **❞**

MAKES ABOUT 3 CUPS
PREP TIME: 10 minutes
COOK TIME: 30 minutes

1¾ cups fresh or frozen
   strawberries

⅔ cup sugar

Peel of 1 lemon

1 cup heavy cream

1 cup milk

Preheat the oven to 350°F. Place the strawberries in a baking pan and toss with the sugar and the lemon peel.

Bake until the sugar has dissolved and it starts to smell quite jammy, about 20 minutes. Add the cream and bake for another 8 to 10 minutes. Remove from the oven and let cool.

Remove the lemon peel and place the mixture in a blender. Add the milk and blend until very smooth. Place in the fridge and let cool completely. Transfer to an ice-cream maker and process according to the manufacturer's instructions. Store in the freezer for up to 1 month.

Marsala Sambayón with Strawberries

Ari Schor

66 If you grew up with good, homemade food, you tend to cook a lot from memory. You push yourself to replicate dishes as you remember them. You often fail, beat yourself up a bit, throw a fit, get lonely, cool off, and call your mom. At least I do. So it makes sense that one of the two desserts on our opening menu at Beba was based on one of my mom's classics: a sambayón (or sabayón or zabaglione) set with a touch of gelatin and served in a mould with a layer of marsala-soaked ladyfinger cookies. Except it was peak strawberry season, so we made the sambayón without the gelatin and chilled it, then served it over the berries and added another childhood favourite of mine: amaretti cookies. 99

SERVES 4
PREP TIME: 10 minutes + 3 hours chilling
COOK TIME: 15 minutes

4 egg yolks

½ cup + 1 tbsp sugar

⅔ cup marsala

⅔ cup whipping cream

4 cups ripe, juicy, perfect, beautiful, summer, accept-no-substitutes Quebec strawberries, at room temperature

12 amaretti cookies, crushed

The tricky part of this recipe is making the base, which is cooked over a water bath. All you need is a small pot of simmering water and a slightly larger heatproof bowl whose lip extends past the edges of the pot.

Bring the small pot of water to a simmer. Place the egg yolks and sugar in the bowl and whisk together for 1 minute. The mixture should lighten in colour. Add the marsala and place the bowl just over the pot of gently simmering water but not touching the water. Whisk over the heat until the mixture foams up and doubles in size. It's a bit of a pain in the ass to do it by hand, so if you have one of those electric beaters, you'll now be glad you schlepped it around for half your life. A digital food thermometer is your best friend here. You want the mixture to reach 180°F, which is the temperature at which egg yolk proteins coagulate.

Remove the bowl from the heat and let cool to room temperature.

In a separate bowl, whip the cream to stiff peaks. Fold the whipped cream into the egg and marsala mixture. Transfer to an airtight container and chill for 3 hours.

Remove the stems from the strawberries and cut the berries in half. Divide the berries between four glasses or bowls. Top with a generous amount of the sambayón and sprinkle with the crushed amaretti cookies. Adults, drink Champagne with this. Trust me.

Hangop with Summer Berry Compote

Hidde Zomer

“ *Hangop* is Dutch for "hang up." It is yogurt that's been thickened by straining out the watery part—the whey—through cheesecloth. Typically, this reduces the volume of the yogurt by half and concentrates the flavour nicely. Alternating the hangop with layers of berry compote makes for a beautifully simple, summery dessert. At home we make this with our boys—they love it. (A more grown-up version might include a drizzle of crème de cassis over the top.) As a young boy in Holland, I used to go with my dad and brother to pick wild berries in the dunes near Bloemendaal. We would bring our haul back to my grandmother, who would incorporate the berries into her hangop. It is one of my fondest memories. And here we are now in the similarly named Bloomfield, in Prince Edward County, doing the same with our little guys, except instead of hunting in dunes, we forage berries that grow wild all around our property. Hangop can also be enjoyed as breakfast by adding fresh berries and crunchy muesli, or oats, and topping it with a generous swirl of honey. **”**

SERVES 4

PREP TIME: 20 minutes + 8 hours (to overnight) chilling

HANGOP

4 cups plain yogurt

1 vanilla bean

⅔ cup heavy cream

¼ cup sugar

SUMMER BERRY COMPOTE

4 cups summer berries, any mix of your choice (the more the merrier)

2 sheets gelatin

3 tbsp sugar

¼ cup water

1 tsp lemon juice, if needed

TO SERVE

4 ladyfingers or other long cookies, for dipping

MAKE THE HANGOP: Rinse a tea towel or large piece of cheesecloth under cold running water. Wring out the excess water and lay the towel or cheesecloth over a colander placed in a large bowl. Transfer the yogurt to the towel or cloth, cover with plastic wrap, and place in the fridge for at least 8 hours, or overnight, making sure there is enough space underneath the colander for the whey to drain away from the yogurt and into the bowl.

When the yogurt has drained, carefully transfer from the towel or cloth to a clean bowl. It should resemble a fresh cheese. Discard the whey.

Slice the vanilla bean in half and scrape the seeds into the yogurt. Whisk to combine.

In a medium bowl, whisk the cream and sugar together until stiff peaks form. Fold the whipped cream into the yogurt until combined. Transfer to an airtight container and refrigerate until ready to serve (see Note on page 234). The mixture will keep for 4 days.

MAKE THE SUMMER BERRY COMPOTE: Place a large ceramic dish in the fridge.

Prepare the berries by stemming, and cutting them as needed to make them the same size.

Place the sheets of gelatin in a bowl of cold water. Let them soak until they are soft.

Continued

In a heavy saucepan over medium heat, bring the sugar and water to a boil. Add the berries and reduce the heat to low, slowly bringing them to a simmer. Once the berries start to release their juice and have softened slightly but have not begun to break down, remove the pot from the heat. Taste the berries and add lemon juice if they are missing some acidity.

Gently squeeze the gelatin sheets, removing the excess water, and add them to the berries. Stir to combine.

Pour the berry mixture into the prepared ceramic dish and let cool until it begins to set. Let chill and fully set in the fridge. The compote will keep in the fridge for up to 1 week.

TO SERVE: Spoon 1 inch of the yogurt mixture into four wide-mouthed mason jars or glasses. Top with 1 inch of the berry compote. Repeat each layer once more. Serve with ladyfingers or similar cookies for dipping. Smakelijk eten!

NOTE: Both the yogurt mixture and compote are best made a day ahead of serving so they have enough time to chill and fully set in the fridge.

Mango Sticky Rice

Nuit Regular

“ Raised in Canada, my kids have naturally grown up surrounded by Canadian culture, and I wanted to ensure that they also have an understanding and appreciation of their Thai culture. My kids, Phai and Marlee, weren't always interested in learning to cook when they were younger, but they always loved to eat mango sticky rice, and I used this dessert as a way to bond with them in the kitchen and teach them about my Thai roots and culture.

Mango sweet sticky rice is a very popular Thai dessert featuring ripened mangoes served with steamed sticky rice in a sweet coconut sauce. In Thailand, it is typically sweetened with cane sugar, but I have adapted my recipe here to use maple syrup to honour my now adopted homeland of Canada too. I especially love using Ataúlfo mangoes—they are super sweet when ripe and aren't too fibrous. During peak peach season in the summertime, you can substitute the mangoes with ripe local peaches. When both mangoes and peaches are out of season, you can use canned mangoes or peaches in a pinch—just make sure to drain the fruit well before using. ”

SERVES 4

PREP TIME: 10 minutes + 3 hours (to overnight) soaking + 20 minutes resting

COOK TIME: 25 minutes

1 cup white glutinous rice

5 cups warm water

1½ cups coconut milk

⅓ cup maple syrup

¼ tsp salt

2 tsp cornstarch

4 ripe, sweet mangoes, peeled and cubed

Place the rice in a medium bowl and cover with 2 cups of the water. Let stand at room temperature for at least 3 hours, or up to overnight, to soften the rice.

Drain and rinse the rice under warm running water for 1 minute. Set aside.

Fill a steamer pot with the remaining 3 cups of water. Bring to a boil over high heat. Line the steamer with cheesecloth or a clean tea towel to prevent the rice from falling through the steamer and place over the boiling water. Turn off the heat and carefully place the rice in the steamer using a large spoon or ladle. Spread the rice out evenly. Turn the heat back to high.

Once the steam starts to rise through the rice, cover the pot with a lid. Turn the heat down to medium and let steam for 20 minutes.

Meanwhile, place 1 cup of the coconut milk in a small saucepan and bring to a boil. Reduce the heat to medium and add the maple syrup and salt. Simmer for 3 minutes, stirring occasionally. Transfer to a medium bowl and set aside.

In the same saucepan, whisk together the remaining coconut milk and the cornstarch. Place over medium heat and simmer, stirring frequently, until the mixture is thickened, about 1 to 2 minutes. Turn off the heat and set aside.

Once the rice is fully cooked, transfer it to the bowl with the coconut maple sauce and stir to combine. Cover the bowl with plastic wrap and let rest, covered, for for 15 minutes. Using a large spoon or spatula, flip the rice over and let rest, covered, for another 5 minutes.

Divide the sticky rice between four plates (or see page 238 for more ideas). Drizzle with the coconut cream and top with the mangoes. Enjoy!

Continued

TRY FUN PLATING IDEAS: The great thing about sticky rice is that it holds its shape, so you can let your kids get creative! Make sticky rice faces by creating perfect circles of sticky rice with a 3- or 4-inch cookie cutter and letting your kids build their own—eyebrows, nose, mouth, hair, etc.—with small cut-up pieces of mango. They can also "paint" the coconut cream topping on or around the mango sticky rice faces. Or, try shaping the rice into animal shapes, and letting your kids use small pieces of mango to decorate their animals or to build a scene on their plate. You can also cut slivers of fresh mango and roll them into rose-like shapes to decorate your sticky rice with—like I did for the photos opposite—if you're feeling fancy.

NOTE: To make it extra fun, you can add food colouring to the rice and/or the coconut cream topping. If you're colouring the rice, use white cane sugar instead of maple syrup and add the food colouring to the sweetened coconut sauce, then proceed with stirring in the rice as directed above.

Oven-Candied Fruit

Caroline Dumas

66 This is the best way to use fruit that looks a little past its best. By cooking them just enough, you really get to savour the notes from each one. And it's such a versatile recipe, because you can use all kinds of fruit, and it pleases even the littlest eaters—especially over ice cream! **99**

MAKES ABOUT 2 CUPS
PREP TIME: 5 minutes
COOK TIME: 25 minutes

1 Italian plum, halved
(no need to remove the pit)

1 peach, halved

1 pear, halved

1 apple, halved

1 quince, quartered

1 orange, sliced

2 figs, halved

1 cup water, as needed

Sugar, as needed

Preheat the oven to 425°F. Place the fruit skin-side down on a baking sheet. Add enough water to just cover the surface of the baking sheet. You don't want to drown the fruit; you just want to prevent over-caramelization. Sprinkle with a bit of sugar.

Cover the baking sheet with aluminum foil and bake for 15 minutes. Carefully remove the foil and turn the fruit skin-side up. Sprinkle with a bit of sugar and bake, covered in foil again, for another 10 minutes. Place on a cooling rack and let cool. Remove any pits.

Serve as a topping for ice cream. For adults it's delicious with a plum liqueur. Store the candied fruit in an airtight container in the fridge for up to 3 days.

Clockwise from top left: Candy Sangria, page 241;
Horchata, page 243; Strawberry Mint Mocktail, page 242

Candy Sangria

Chanthy Yen

I, like so many people, had candy growing up. Today there are more options to our childhood favourites filled with concentrated additives and extracts, like all-natural gummies that have no artificial flavours or colouring. This recipe is a fun way to make something big out of a small packet of any type of candy. Whether you are camping or enjoying a backyard barbecue, your kids will love this drink. Serve it on ice with a few berries or slices of citrus fruit and it's bound to make anyone happy. Brace yourself for the sugar rush.

MAKES 4 CUPS; SERVES 4
PREP TIME: 10 minutes

1 (100 g/3.5 oz) bag of
   your favourite candy

1 cup boiling water

4 cups ice cubes

2 cups cold water

1 cup berries or citrus slices

Fruit juice (optional)

Place the candy in a heatproof mason jar. Add the boiling water and stir to dissolve the candy. Place the ice cubes in a pitcher and add the cold water, fruit, and candied water. Feel free to spice it up with the fruit juice of your choice. Adults can add wine and enjoy.

Strawberry Mint Mocktail

Véronique Rivest

66 When my husband and I would have drinks before dinner, I would ask the kids, "Who wants a cocktail?" The kids loved to get a drink coming out of a shaker, all frothy and colourful, even if it was just orange and cranberry juice with ice.

The base for many cocktails, alcoholic or not, is simple syrup. Great cocktails, just like great wine, are all about balance. Simple syrup brings sweetness to the equation. It is the easiest thing to make: bring equal parts of water and sugar to a boil, stir until the sugar is dissolved, and let cool. That's it! But the fun part is that you can flavour simple syrup with all kinds of herbs, fruits, or spices. I always have a few flavoured syrups handy to make simple, fast, and tasty non-alcoholic drinks: Simply combine a flavoured simple syrup, with some more fruit or herbs, and some soda water. One of my particular favourites is strawberry simple syrup, which I combine here with fresh mint leaves, a little lime, and soda water.

One of the great things about this mocktail is making kids aware of what they eat and drink. So many ready-made drinks are packed with additives of all kinds; making your own allows you to know exactly what you're drinking, and also to adapt the recipes to your taste. Source great-quality ingredients and let those shine. 99

MAKES 1 DRINK
PREP TIME: 10 minutes
COOK TIME: 5 minutes

STRAWBERRY SIMPLE SYRUP

2½ cups halved strawberries
   (or raspberries)

1 cup sugar

1 cup water

MOCKTAIL

½ lime, quartered (before cutting,
   roll the lime over a hard surface
   to release the juice)

8 fresh mint leaves

3 to 4 tbsp (1.5 to 2 oz) strawberry
   simple syrup

Ice cubes

Soda water

MAKE THE STRAWBERRY SIMPLE SYRUP: In a medium saucepan over medium-high heat, combine all the ingredients. Bring to a boil, stirring to dissolve the sugar, and let simmer for 5 minutes. Break up the fruit using a wooden spoon or whisk. Remove from the heat and let cool. Strain through a fine-mesh sieve, discarding any solids, and transfer to a glass jar or bottle. Seal and store in the fridge for up to 3 to 4 weeks.

MAKE THE MOCKTAIL: In a cocktail shaker, muddle the lime and mint. Add the simple syrup, fill the glass with ice cubes, and top with soda water. Stir together and pour into a highball glass.

Photo on page 240

Horchata

Sandra Soto

" Growing up, my mother never gave us soda. This refreshing drink was always a part of our dinner, either made this way, using rice, or sometimes using fresh fruit, like watermelon and lime instead, and a little sugar. **"**

SERVES 4 TO 6

PREP TIME: 5 minutes + overnight chilling

1½ cups jasmine rice

2 cinnamon sticks

1 tbsp vanilla

½ cup lightly packed brown sugar, or more to taste

6 cups water

Ice cubes, to serve

Photo on page 240

Place the rice, cinnamon sticks, vanilla, and sugar in a large container and cover with half of the water. Place in the fridge and chill overnight.

The following day, transfer the mixture to a blender and blend until smooth, about 3 minutes. Strain through a fine-mesh sieve lined with cheesecloth, pressing on the solids to extract all the liquid. Adjust the sweetness to taste, add the remaining water, and serve over ice. Store in the fridge for up to 3 days.

The Chefs

Lisa Ahier is a chef and restaurateur who honed her craft in the United States before opening her restaurant on the West Coast of Canada. She is the co-author of *The SoBo Cookbook*. sobo.ca; @lisaahier

Billy Alexander is an Indigenous chef, tourism ambassador, cultural pundit, and social advocate. As Director of Programs at the Culinary Tourism Alliance, he is part of a movement to bring people together through culinary experiences and stories. culinarytourismalliance.com; @culinarytourismalliance

Angus An is a chef and restaurateur who trained at Michelin-starred restaurants before opening his restaurants in Vancouver. He is the author of *Maenam*. maenam.ca; @chefangusan

Suzanne Barr is a chef, social advocate, speaker, and TV personality who promotes a healthier kitchen culture. She is the author of *My Ackee Tree*, a memoir and collection of keepsake recipes. suzannebarrfood.com; @suzanne_barr_food

Maha Barsoom is a chef and restaurateur who has been cooking authentic Egyptian cuisine for more than 40 years. She runs her restaurant with her daughter and son, serving the best Egyptian food, coffee and tea in Toronto. mahasbrunch.com; @mahabarsoom

Christa Bruneau-Guenther is a chef and TV personality who focuses on celebrating Indigenous techniques and recipes. Her recipes have been featured in magazines like *Canadian Living* and *Chatelaine*. feastcafebistro.com; @christaguenther; @feastcafebistro

Mehdi Brunet-Benkritly and Molly Superfine-Rivera met while both working in restaurants in New York City and came back to Mehdi's hometown of Montreal to open up their own restaurant, Marconi, and more recently, Mollies, a country style diner in Sutton, Quebec. marconimontreal.com; @marconimontreal; @mollies.dinette.sutton

Andrea Callan is a chef, culinary cannabis director, general manager, and gardener who has experience cooking at some of Canada's best wineries. @chefsimplicity

Emma Cardarelli is a chef and restaurateur who worked her way up through some of Montreal's best kitchens before opening her own restaurants devoted to highlighting the beauty of regional Italian cuisine. noragray.com; @nonnanora

Jeremy Charles is a chef and advocate for preserving a unique Newfoundland cuisine. He is the co-author of *Wildness*. @jeremy_charles77

Alex Chen is a chef and culinary competitor. He has represented Canada in some of the world's most prestigious cooking competitions. boulevardvancouver.com; @chefalexchen

Jonathan Cheung is a cookbook store owner and culinary instructor with years of experience as a chef. He is the co-author of *Montreal Cooks*. appetitebooks.ca; @appetite4books

Derek Dammann is a chef and restaurateur with experience in restaurants in Victoria, B.C, London, England, and everywhere in between. He is the co-author of *True North*. maisonpublique.com; @maisonpublique

Ralph Alerte Desamours & Lee-Anne Millaire Lafleur

are restaurateurs from Montreal who bring tropical flavours to the food scene. After working in the Caribbean and Latin America, they created a menu inspired by all the countries that have palm trees. restopalme.ca; @resto_palme

Connie DeSousa & John Jackson

are chefs, restaurateurs, mentors & leaders in Canada's restaurant industry. The award-winning CHARCUT Roast House is their flagship restaurant among many other destination restaurants across the Canadian Prairies. charcut.com; @charcut; @conniedesousa

Jennifer Dewasha is a chef and

culinary instructor. She spent a lifetime learning how to prepare meticulous French cuisine and now spends her time teaching the next generation of chefs. thesmokinbirds.com; @thesmokinbirds; @jdewasha

Meeru Dhalwala is a chef, restaurateur,

and agent for change in Canada's food community. She has written and created recipes for three cookbooks, including *Vij's Indian*. vijs.ca; @meerudhalwala

Vincent Dion Lavallée is a chef,

restaurateur, and cider maker whose cooking celebrates the culinary heritage of Quebec. aupieddecochon.ca; @v_lavallee

Aman Dosanj is a former footballer and

current marketing whiz turned chef, culinary entrepreneur, and food writer who also runs a series of pop-up dinners. paisleynotebook.com; @paisleynotebook

Luc Doucet is a chef and restaurateur

who uses his cooking to help develop the local food community in New Brunswick. blackrabbit. restaurant; @blackrabbitmct; @lucdoucetmct

Caroline Dumas is a chef, restaurateur,

founder of Soupesoup, and entrepreneur. She is the author of multiple books, including *Caro Keto*. restaurantbloomfield.com; @caroline.dumas

Anita Feng is a chef and restaurateur

who operates several food concepts in Montreal, exploring regional Chinese cuisine, particularly the food of the Sichuan province. jaifengmtl.com; @jai.feng.mtl; @anitaymfeng

Marie Fitrion is a CEO for Urban Acorn

Catering, food enthusiast, and freelance writer whose stories about food explores her Haitian and Scottish heritage. voodoohaggis.com; @voodoohaggisstories

Tita Flips is a chef and restaurateur known

for supplying Toronto's diners with excellent Filipino street food. titaflips.com; @titaflips

Michele Forgione is a chef, restaurateur,

entrepreneur, and TV personality. Whether through his restaurants or his grocery products, he is working to celebrate quality Italian ingredients. impastomtl.ca; @micheleforgione

Sarah Forrester is a chef, caterer, and

restaurateur specializing in serving macrobiotic foods to suit vegan and vegetarian diets. macromom.ca; @macromomwholefoods

Adrian Forte is a chef, restaurateur, and

TV personality known for his signature take on Afro-Caribbean cuisine. He is the author of *Yawd*. yawd.ca; @adrianforte

Raquel Fox is a chef, an award-winning

cookbook author, former restaurateur, and Caribbean culinary instructor. islandgurlfoods.com; @islandgurlfoods

Joe Friday is a chef, restaurateur, and

entrepreneur who trained in kitchens around the globe before returning to Canada to open several successful restaurants. chefjoefriday.com; @chefjoefriday

Dan Geltner is a private chef, caterer, and restaurant consultant who helps bring people's dream food concepts to life. He has contributed to many of Montreal's best restaurants. dangeltner.com; @chefdangeltner

Rob Gentile is a chef, restaurateur, entrepreneur, and TV personality known for his expansive knowledge of Italian cuisine. @rob_gentile

Ryan Gray is a restaurateur who worked in some of Montreal's best restaurants before opening his own. He is the wine director and co-owner of Nora Gray, Elena, and Gia Vin & Grill. coffeepizzawine.com; giagiagia.com; noragray.com; @noragrayresto; @giagiagiamtl; @ryangraymtl

David Gunawan is a chef and restaurateur who learned to cook at Michelin-starred kitchens across Europe before arriving in Vancouver to open several restaurants. ubuntucanteen.ca; @mas_leche_por_favor

Katie & Shane Hayes are chefs and restaurateurs celebrating local Newfoundland ingredients after a career spent travelling the world. bonavistasocialclub.com; @thebonavistasocialclub

Rogelio Herrera is a chef and restaurateur who cooked in kitchens around the world before bringing his talents to Canada. alloydining.com; @alloydining; @rogeliochef

Nick Hodge is a chef, restaurateur, and farmer. He uses many of the products he grows on his farms in the food he serves in his restaurant in Montreal. @icehousemtl

Chuck Hughes is a chef, restaurateur, and TV personality. He is the author of several books, including *Chuck's Day Off*. chuckhughes.ca; @chefchuckhughes

Emilia Jamieson is a chef, baker, and restaurateur who is best known for her vegan and gluten-free creations at Lu & I in Montreal. @emiliabakes; @lu.and.i

Michelle Jobin is a TV personality, spokesperson, and podcast host. In addition to her coverage of all things food, she is a passionate home cook. michellejobin.com; @michelle.jobin

Lora Kirk is a chef, restaurateur, consultant, and food activist who champions the local food movement. She is the co-author of *Hearth & Home*. @chef_lora

Stéphanie Labelle is a pastry chef who blends classic pastry techniques with modern flavours to create a style of pastries that is all her own. patisserierhubarbe.com; @rhubarbe_mtl

Renée Lavallée is a chef, TV personality, and culinary competitor who has competed in some of the world's most prestigious culinary competitions. thecanteen.ca; @feistychef

Susur Lee is a chef, restaurateur, and TV personality who has opened restaurants around the world. He makes frequent appearances on food television in Canada and the United States. susur.com; @susurlee

Celeste Mah is a pastry chef whose specialty is incorporating staples of the Newfoundland pantry into world-class desserts. @cellymaemah

Cat McInroy is a chef, baker, and culinary instructor who started cooking on her days off as an RCMP first responder. She created the only culinary school in northern Canada that teaches home cooks. wellbread.ca; @yukonchef

David McMillan is a chef and restaurateur who worked his way up the ranks of some of Montreal's most well-regarded kitchens. He is the co-author of two books, most recently *Joe Beef: Surviving the Apocalypse*. hayfieldfarm.ca; @hayfieldfarm

Fred Morin is a chef and restaurateur who worked his way up the ranks of some of Montreal's most well-regarded kitchens. He is the co-author of two books, most recently *Joe Beef: Surviving the Apocalypse*. joebeef.com; @fredmadeit

Ryusuke Nakagawa is a chef who honed his craft of kaiseki at Michelin-starred restaurants in Japan. His modern interpretation of kaiseki cuisine uses contemporary and ancient techniques to highlight premium Japanese ingredients and local produce. aburihana.com; @ryusuke_nakagawa

Brian Ng left his life as a civil servant to follow his dream to become a chef and restaurateur. He takes inspiration from the unique local ingredients available in the Yukon. wayfareroysterhouse.com; @thefinishline1

Jessica Noël is a chef who has spent time cooking in restaurants in Montreal, New York, and Europe before returning to Montreal to lead the kitchen with Marc-Olivier Frappier at Vin Mon Lapin. vinmonlapin.com; @jessicaxmas

Tara O'Brady is a food writer, TV personality, and food consultant who regularly contributes to national food publications. She is the author of *Seven Spoons*. taraobrady.com; @taraobrady

Anna Olson is a chef, baker, and TV personality recognized as "Canada's baking sweetheart." She has written several books, most recently *Baking Day with Anna Olson*. annaolson.ca; @chefannaolson

J-C Poirier is a chef and restaurateur dedicated to bringing the taste of Quebec to the West Coast. He is the author of *Where the River Narrows*. stlawrencerestaurant.com; @jcpoirier

Nuit Regular is a Toronto-based chef and restaurateur who has been honoured by the Royal Thai Government for her contributions to Thai cooking in Canada. She is the author of the award-winning cookbook *Kiin*. bychefnuit.com; @chefnuitregular

Véronique Rivest is a sommelier, wine writer, restaurateur, and TV and radio personality. She has been instrumental in the growth of Canada's wine culture. veroniquerivest.com; @veroniquerivest

Anthony Rose is a chef and restaurateur who cooked in Michelin-starred kitchens in the United States before returning to Toronto to open some of the city's favourite restaurants. He is the co-author of *The Last Schmaltz*. wilderandrose.com; @chefanthonyrose

Amy Rosen is a James Beard Award-nominated journalist, editor, and cinnamon bun expert. She is the author of five books, including *Kosher Style*. amyrosen.com; @amyrrosen

Ari Schor is a chef and restaurateur who cooked in some of Montreal's best kitchens before earning praise for his cuisine influenced by his Argentine roots. shopbeba.ca; @donlardo

Katie Shmelinski is a baker and restaurateur known for her one-of-a-kind sourdough doughnuts. theeverydaykitchen.ca; @theeverydaykatie; @theeverydaykitchen

Danny Smiles is a chef and TV personality. He is a stalwart of the Montreal restaurant scene, known for his creative, flavourful dishes using local ingredients and influenced by his Quebec upbringing along with his Italian and Egyptian roots. aubergewillowinn.com; @chefdannysmiles

Michael Smith is a chef and TV personality who celebrates the bounty of Prince Edward Island. He is the author of 11 cookbooks, including *Farm, Fire & Feast*. innatbayfortune.com; @chefmichaelsmith

Dyan Solomon is a chef and restaurateur known for her Montreal restaurants that provide the perfect destination for every meal. She is the author of *Olive + Gourmando*. oliveetgourmando.com; @dyansolomon

Sandra Soto is a chef and restaurateur known for their popular takes on traditional Mexican street food. @sansoto

Raegan Steinberg is a chef and restaurateur who worked at several Montreal restaurants before opening her own, known for serving Montreal's best comfort food. arthursmtl.com; @raegssmtl

Joe Thottungal is a chef, restaurateur, and culinary competitor specializing in South Indian cuisine. He is the author of *Coconut Lagoon*. coconutlagoon.ca; @coconutlagoon_joe

Kim Thúy worked in many different fields, including as a seamstress, lawyer, and interpreter, before becoming a world-renowned author. She is the author of multiple works of fiction and one cookbook, *Secrets from My Vietnamese Kitchen*. kimthuy.ca; @kimthuylythanh

Janice Tiefenbach is a founding member of Concordia University's Peoples Potato, and can now be found as Executive Chef of Montreal's Italian restaurants Elena and Gia Vin & Grill. coffeepizzawine.com; @elenamontreal; @giagiagiamtl

Paul Toussaint is a chef and restaurateur who uses his various restaurant concepts to present the culinary favourites of his Caribbean culture. kamuy.ca; @chefpaultoussaint

Lloyd Tull is a chef, restaurateur, and Jamaican patty magnate. He is beloved in Montreal for supplying the city with perfect renditions of Caribbean culinary classics. lloydies.ca; @lloydies.mtl

Vikram Vij is a chef, restaurateur, and TV personality well known for blending Indian spices with local meats, fish, and produce. He is the author of *Vij*. vijs.ca; @chefvikramvij

Cory Vitiello is a chef, culinary director, and restaurateur who has helped open several popular restaurant concepts across Canada. eatflock.com; @coryvitiello

Robin Wasicuna is an Indigenous chef, TV personality, and restaurateur known for serving some of the best comfort food in Yellowknife. He has contributed recipes to three books, including *Feast*. @feedfirenourishsoul

Mandy & Rebecca Wolfe are the co-owners of Mandy's, a collection of popular gourmet-salad restaurants in Montreal and Toronto. They are the co-authors of *Mandy's Gourmet Salads* and *More Mandy's*. shop.mandys.ca; @mandysalads

Camilla Wynne is a writer, recipe developer, cooking teacher, and one of Canada's only Master Preservers. She is the author of *Jam Bake* and *Preservation Society Home Preserves*. camillawynne.com; @camillawynne

Chanthy Yen is a Cambodian-Canadian chef and restaurateur who has worked in restaurants from coast to coast ever since arriving in the city after years spent cooking in Europe's finest kitchens. tiramisumtl.com; @chanthyyen

Hidde Zomer is a chef and restaurateur, originally from the Netherlands, who now practises his unique style of live-fire cooking in Prince Edward County, Ontario. flameandsmith.com; @chefhidde

Acknowledgments

This book was a massive undertaking that spanned years of hard work, and it wouldn't have been possible without the talent and generosity of our Canadian culinary community, the help—and patience—of many skillful people, and the constant encouragement of family and friends.

First and foremost, thank you to my incredible editor at Appetite, Lindsay Paterson, for believing in this idea, convincing me not to give up in the darkest days of the early pandemic, and being a support and sounding board for me every step of the way. Thank you to Robert McCullough for taking a chance on me, and the entire Appetite team for bringing these pages to life.

I could not have done this cookbook without the help of my insanely talented photographer and friend, Dominique Lafond, whose critical eye and effortless style I am so grateful for. Thank you to the wonderful Maya Visnyei in Toronto and Viranlly Liemena in Vancouver for helping me shoot chefs in those cities when travelling from Montreal was restricted.

Thank you, Michelle Marek, for your invaluable recipe editing and testing, and your culinary skills. Amie Watson, I could not have figured out all my spreadsheets, and contacted and kept track of so many chefs alone—you were an essential part of this project. Roxanne Chagnon, you understood my vision and provided me with the perfect kitchen props, dishware, and backdrops to shoot these recipes. Thank you to my agent, Maude-Isabelle Delagrave, for showing me the ropes, and thank you to fellow cookbook writer Meredith Erickson for giving me the confidence to take this project on, and for introducing me to Lindsay. And thank you to Fred Morin for his continued support and who, when I first told him the premise of this book, replied "Yeah, that's actually a really good idea."

Without the chefs, there would be no cookbook. So, to everyone from coast to coast who actually said yes to this endeavour, and then continued to answer my emails and questions for almost three years after the initial ask, I am so honoured to have you all in these pages—not only with your recipes, but with your heartwarming, touching, personal stories about cooking for your kids. To those who were gracious enough to let us come into your homes (or yards), I cannot thank you enough for sharing your family with me.

Making a book about cooking for kids when you are not allowed to gather, be in groups, or have parties was the ultimate challenge. So, thank you to my family, and close friends for lending me your little ones for one blissful afternoon in the sun.

Thank you to my parents and mother-in-law for taking on some of the recipe prep when things got a little crazy with the photoshoots. You really saved my ass.

Speaking of photoshoots, one thing the pandemic forced upon us with this endeavour was to make do with what we had and under the circumstances. If we hadn't had to shoot almost all of this book in my home with just Dominique, Michelle, and me, I would have never ventured into my son's nearby toy boxes or mini kitchen in search of fun props. These toys ended up shaping the entire style of this cookbook, making it so unique, and incredibly personal for me.

Which comes to a huge thank you, to my partner, Robb, who was a constant source of support, whether it was going to the store with my endless shopping lists, putting our son to bed so I could work late, or letting me take over our living room, dining room, and kitchen for weeks of shooting—I love you.

Finally, thank you to my son, Fox, not only for being the inspiration for *Little Critics*, but for being my test subject throughout this wild ride, and for teaching me that, when it comes to food, you really never know until you try.

Index